Your Child and JESUS

A Family Activity Book

D1507436

Written by
Rick Osborne
with **Kevin Miller**

Illustrated by **Ken Save**

MOODY PRESS

CHICAGO

Text and Illustrations © 1999 by LIGHTWAVE PUBLISHING INC.

For Lightwave
Managing Editor: *Elaine Osborne*
Text Director: *K. Christie Bowler*
Art Director: *Terry Van Roon*
Desktop: *Andrew Jaster*

All Scripture quotations, unless indicated, are taken from the *Holy Bible: New International Reader's Version*®. NIrV © 1995, 1996, 1998 by International Bible Society. Used by permission of Zondervan Publishing House. All rights reserved.

The "NIrV" and "New International Reader's Version" trademarks are registered in the United States Patent and Trademark Office by International Bible Society. Use of either trademark requires permission of International Bible Society.

ISBN: 0-8024-2855-X

Printed in the United States of America

The Approach

Chapter One

Getting Started

In the Middle of Life

Life can be frantic. There are so many activities to chauffeur the kids to, pay fees for, and organize. How can you find the time and energy to discipline your children wisely, oversee their manners, show them love, and assist them in developing a relationship with Jesus? The task is daunting. But the answer is simpler than you may think: Teach and train your children right in the midst of life! Effective training is a matter of mind-set and attitude. It's as simple as 1 - 2 - 3 - 4: (1) Understand the topic, (2) Live out your understanding, (3) Communicate the topic, and (4) Help with application. All of this can happen right in the middle of life. That's great, because life is exactly what you're teaching.

Two-Part Learning

No one can learn anything practical through *teaching* alone. Would you trust a dentist who had only read books? A dentist must know how teeth are made, but he must also know how to use a drill. In the same way, a Christian must know who Jesus is and what He said and did, but that's not enough.

The other crucial part of learning is *training*: the hands-on application of what is learned. Dentists must practice taking X-rays and doing fillings. Christians must apply the teachings and character traits of Jesus to their lives. Otherwise, the knowledge is purposeless. Teaching and training are best done together. This happens in life as teachable, trainable moments present themselves.

Seize the Moment

In the middle of your responsibilities and commitments, planning times to impart knowledge to your children and to train them to apply it seems like just one more pressure. But that doesn't have to be true. Life is happening all around you whether you plan it or not. And every life event is a ready-made opportunity to teach and train your children. The key is recognizing the moment. God referred to this approach when He told the Israelites in Deuteronomy 6:6–9 to use every part of life to teach their children.

Some of the best times to train come when they ask questions or are dealing with problems and their interest is high. When children ask questions, they're primed to learn. Two minutes of solid teaching at that moment will stay with them more than a dozen lectures. Use their interest and curiosity to your advantage. Be on the lookout for that God-given opportunity where teaching and training collide to create a real-life teachable, trainable moment.

They're Watching!

Modeling is another way to teach and train children. They watch what you do in both good and bad times. Don't think you can teach something only if you've mastered it. Watching you learn is a great teaching tool. Children notice your responses to temptation, frustration, windfalls, and shortages. They know more about your honesty, diligence, and money handling than you realize. Do they watch you keep that extra change or gossip about a colleague? Or do they see you return the change, pray for that colleague, or work extra hours without grumbling? Whatever you're doing, they're learning. Guaranteed.

Goal and Principles

The goal of your teaching is to show your children that Jesus is their Lord and Savior. He loves them. This is why God gave them to you to care for—so that you could help them understand this truth. God wants to help you with this. He keeps as involved in your life as you let Him. Here are some effective teaching and training principles to keep in mind as you go through the rest of this book.

Keep It Interesting: Remember to keep your teaching enjoyable and exciting. Ways to do this include modeling, showing love and respect, having fun, making the teaching relevant, using variety, focusing on their questions, and employing the KISS method: "Keep It Simple and Sincere."

Grace Parenting: God has given you the privilege and responsibility of forming your children into wonderful human beings. He has also given you a choice as to how you will go about it. When you choose to

raise your children in partnership with Him and ask for help and wisdom, He is right there with His grace. When you raise your children in harmony with God's principles and how He created everything to work—according to the manufacturer's instructions as it were, and with His toll-free help line constantly open—you have the greatest possibility of success.

Growing Together: It's important to let your children watch you learn. Your mistakes can be the best teaching opportunities as you are open and honest with your children. To say, "I made a mistake. But that's OK because I learned something, too," is to free your children to explore new things without fear of failure. It also shows them that growth is a lifelong adventure, and conveys the idea that you are growing along with them.

Love: How you treat your children will affect them for the rest of their lives. These days we often hear of "inner healing," "repressed memories," "long-term therapy," and all the other ways of healing the results of bad parenting. This focus on the negative effects of parenting can cause parents to feel overwhelmed and perhaps tempt them to neglect discipline and correction in fear of harming their children for life. But God is clear on the need for loving discipline (see Proverbs 3:11–12; 13:24). And the best way to help your children avoid years of therapy in the future is to sow seeds of love now.

Respect: Children are future adults. Having them in your care is a great privilege. From day one, they should be treated the same way other people are treated—with respect, consideration, and politeness. Children have feelings, thoughts, ideas, dreams, and fears just like adults. Their opinions matter. Their questions need to be addressed. Their thoughts should be listened to. Their desires should influence family decisions and house rules. Simple respect will go a long way to help them understand how God values and respects them.

Fun: Laughter and fun make learning enjoyable and memorable. God invented fun and laughter. Be careful not to talk about Him and His ways only when something is wrong. Introduce God into fun times, too. Make learning about God, His Book, and His world a natural, ongoing part of everyday life. Include variety. Approach a topic from different angles. Use all five senses in your learning activities. Lessons that are enjoyed will be remembered.

Using This Book

Why This Book?

Although effective teaching and training can happen in the midst of life, some preparation is needed. You can't grab the moment if you don't have the information ready. Each chapter in this book is designed to help you be ready.

At times we'll encourage you to plan a teachable moment. You can "seed" life and purposely set up opportunities with a few props, actions, and words. These moments can be just as effective as spontaneous ones.

Topic:

We briefly explain the basic biblical teaching on a topic. Much of this may be familiar, but if it's new, take the time to read and understand it. We've organized the teaching in a logical progression to give you a clear grasp of the main points your children will need to learn. Our goal is to enable you to easily and clearly explain the topic in a variety of contexts.

Places to Model It:

Once you've grasped the information, you'll apply it to your own life as your children watch. We give examples of how, where, and when you can live out the material. There are as many different opportunities as there are people. Our goal is to help you recognize and make use of the opportunities in your everyday life.

Tips to Teach It:

This is the heart of the book. First, we give a key Bible verse for your children to memorize in order to keep the chapter's teaching in their heads and hearts. This is followed by a key Bible story and some

discussion questions. Next, we give examples of situations where the chapter's topic can be effectively taught. Some situations can be created with minimal planning. Our goal is for these tips to focus your attention on the myriad opportunities available in your child's life. The situations described are a starting place. Once you're thinking this way, you'll find many others.

Tools to Do It:

We also provide a variety of tools to drive the point home. These include games, trivia, Bible stories, lists, and other resources. When you've used an opportunity life has provided to get into a topic, pull out some of these tools to reinforce and expand your teaching.

Trivia and Jokes:

We have scattered fun jokes and interesting trivia throughout this book. These can be used as discussion starters or just for fun.

Motto:

We provide mottos to help reinforce each chapter's topic. You can use the mottos we suggest or make up some on your own that are unique to your family.

What to Do

With a little preparation you'll be ready to take advantage of the moments God provides.

- Go over the theory until it's clear in your mind.

- Look through the modeling examples. Think of other times and places you can use to teach the concepts to your children.

- Read the teaching tips carefully. You'll recognize other opportunities as they arise. Trust God to show you when you're in the middle of a teachable moment.

- Become familiar with the tools. Learn how the games work and review the Bible stories.

- Finally, pray for God's help in recognizing opportunities, communicating His principles, and making the teaching practical.

Who Is Jesus?

Topic

More Than a Man

Jesus is the center of the Christian faith, but how can you help your children truly know who He is? Well, for one thing, when they ask you who Jesus is, whatever you do, don't tell them that He was just a prophet, a great moral teacher, or a master storyteller, as many people say. That is only part of the story. Jesus is much more than a man. He is God, and He loves them.

Since He first came to earth, people have debated just who Jesus is. The Jewish leaders who arrested Him could see that He was a man, but He also claimed to be God (John 10:33). To the Jews, claiming to be God was blasphemy, so they had Him killed. But is Jesus really God? If you study the wealth of evidence, you must accept this to be true. Jesus is more than a man. He is "God come in the flesh," and He is the most wonderful person the world has ever seen.

A Special Birth

Even though Jesus has always existed as God, He came to earth as a baby. As a member of the Trinity, which includes the Father, the Son (Jesus), and the Holy Spirit, Jesus created everything. He is all-powerful, He knows everything, and He exists everywhere at once. Yet He put all 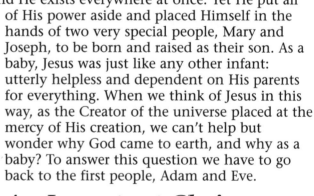 of His power aside and placed Himself in the hands of two very special people, Mary and Joseph, to be born and raised as their son. As a baby, Jesus was just like any other infant: utterly helpless and dependent on His parents for everything. When we think of Jesus in this way, as the Creator of the universe placed at the mercy of His creation, we can't help but wonder why God came to earth, and why as a baby? To answer this question we have to go back to the first people, Adam and Eve.

An Important Choice

When God created human beings, He gave us *free will*. That means we have the ability to either accept or reject His will. God did this because He wanted us to *choose* to love and obey Him, rather than forcing us to submit to Him like mindless robots. But by giving us free will, God also created the possibility for us to make wrong choices and sin—which is exactly what Adam and Eve did. God gave us free will even though He knew that one day He would need to make up for our bad decisions. Like a loving parent, He made Himself responsible for us, including taking care of our mistakes.

Adam and Eve were told not to eat fruit from the tree at the center of the Garden of Eden. If they did, God told them, they would die. Adam and Eve disobeyed God and ate the fruit. This is called sin, and the penalty is death. Since they were the first people, everyone born after them has been born sinful and under a sentence of death, too. However—right when Adam and Eve made their choice—Jesus, who is God, knew He would have to come and die to pay the penalty for our sin. Jesus is the only one who could have died for us, because He is the only sinless person who ever lived. (See chapter 5 for more on this.) Because of Jesus and His death on the cross for us we can have everything: God as our loving Father, the Holy Spirit helping us in our lives, and the chance to live forever with God in heaven.

So when your children ask, "Who is Jesus?" you can tell them that He's much, much more than a man. He is God, and He wants each one of us to know Him personally.

Places to Model It!

- Try to model respect for Jesus through your words and actions. For example, make sure that you never take the Lord's name in vain or use phrases such as "Jesus" or "Oh, God" casually. Instead, speak the name of Jesus as a blessing, and tell your children about His phenomenal love for them.

- Model the loving father-child relationship you have with God by demonstrating the same kind of love and respect to your children. No matter what they say or do, affirm them as people and assure them that your love for them will never fail.

- To help your children identify with Jesus and to show them that Jesus can identify with them, talk about Him as a person who has gone through everything they have— both good times and difficult ones—so He can understand them and their struggles. This fact is particularly important for children to understand because they may fail to realize that Jesus was a child at one time and went through many of the same struggles and trials that they do.

Tips to Teach It!

Key Verse:

"Thomas said to him, 'My Lord and my God!' Then Jesus told him, 'Because you have seen me, you have believed. Blessed are those who have not seen me but still have believed.'" (John 20:28–29)

Key Bible Story:

Although the Jewish religious leaders often opposed Jesus for what He did, they were much more concerned with who He claimed to be: the Son of God, which was the same as claiming to be God (see John 5:18). To them, this claim was blasphemy and was punishable by death. Read John 10:22–33 with your children and discuss the following questions.

- Why didn't the Jews believe that Jesus was the Christ?

- Who are the sheep that Jesus talks about?

- Why did the Jews want to stone Jesus?

Teachable Moments

- When you're praying with your family at the dinner table, take a moment to explain why you say "In Jesus' name" at the end of your prayers. (Because He made it possible for you to have a relationship with God again.) Encourage your children to put the phrase "In Jesus' name" into their own words, such as "Because Jesus loves us so much," or "Because Jesus died for us," so that they can better understand what it means.

- When a baby is born in the family or when you and your children see a baby, use the moment to reinforce how helpless and innocent Jesus was when He was born and that He was once a baby, just as they were.

- During Christmas and Easter, when people are talking about the birth, life, death, and resurrection of Jesus, emphasize to your children that these events really happened and how truly amazing they are. Talk to them about what an incredible sacrifice Jesus made for them.

- When you're out in nature, talk about how Jesus, as God, made all the beauty you are enjoying.

MOTTO

Jesus is God, and I will follow Him.

Tools to Do It!

1 Quotes About Jesus

When Jesus Christ came to earth, He changed the world. He accomplished that feat, and still accomplishes it every day, by impacting the lives of individual people. Here's what some people have said about Jesus and His effect on their lives:

IN JESUS' NAME...

IN JESUS' AWESOME, WONDERFUL NAME!

- "What kind of man is this? Even the winds and the waves obey him!"

  –Jesus' disciples (Matthew 8:27)

- "If Shakespeare should come into this room, we would all rise; but if Jesus Christ should come in, we would all kneel."

  –Charles Lamb, writer

- "Here is a man who was born in an obscure village, the child of a peasant woman. He grew up in another obscure village. He worked in a carpenter shop until He was thirty, and then for three years He was an itinerant preacher.

  He never wrote a book. He never held an office. He never owned a home. He never had a family.

  He never went to college. He never put His foot inside a big city. He never travelled two hundred miles from the place where He was born. He never did any of the things that usually accompany greatness.

  He had no credentials but Himself. He had nothing to do with this world except the naked power of His divine manhood. While still a young man, the tide of popular opinion turned against Him.

  His friends ran away. One of them denied Him. He was turned over to His enemies. He went through the mockery of a trial.

  He was nailed to a cross between two thieves. His executioners gambled for the only piece of property He had on earth while He was dying—and that was His coat. When He was dead He was taken down and laid in a borrowed grave through the pity of a friend.

  Nineteen wide centuries have come and gone and today He is the centerpiece of the human race and the leader of the column of progress.

I am far within the mark when I say that all the armies that ever marched, and all the navies that ever were built, and all the parliaments that ever sat, and all the kings that ever reigned, put together have not affected the life of man upon this earth as powerfully as has that One solitary life!"

–James A. Francis, D. D.

2 Explaining the Trinity

The Bible teaches us that God is one, but He exists as three persons: God the Father, Jesus the Son, and the Holy Spirit. This understanding of God is called "the Trinity." The following "kid friendly" explanations of the Trinity will help you to explain it to your children.

- Consider Jesus' baptism (Matthew 3:16–17). Jesus the *Son* was in the water, the *Spirit* came down like a dove, and the *Father* spoke from heaven. God is three persons—Father, Son, and Holy Spirit. God is all three at the same time, and They're all God. They're not parts of God. All three share the same nature: They all fill everything, know everything, and can do anything. There is nothing They don't share. Therefore, They're one and the same God. So what makes Them three? Their persons and Their jobs.

  God is our Father. He is the source and creator of everything: *"But for us there is only one God. He is the Father. All things came from him, and we live for him"* (1 Corinthians 8:6).

  God the Son, Jesus, died to save us from our sins: *"Here is how God has shown his love for us. While we were still sinners, Christ died for us"* (Romans 5:8). He is the head or leader of all Christians: *"Christ is the head of the church. The church is Christ's body. He is its Savior"* (Ephesians 5:23). And He will eventually judge us: *"Also, the Father does not judge anyone. He has given the Son the task of judging"* (John 5:22).

  God the Holy Spirit is always with us: *"I will ask the Father. And he will give you another Friend to help you and to be with you forever. The Friend is the Spirit of truth. The world can't accept him. That is because the world does not see him or know him. But you know him. He lives with you, and he will be in you"* (John 14:16–17). He teaches us and helps us become more like Jesus: *"But the Father will send the Friend in my name to help you. The Friend is the Holy Spirit. He will teach you all things. He will remind you of everything I have said to you"* (John 14:26).

- Two other things that can be used to explain the Trinity are eggs and water. An egg has three separate and distinct parts: the shell, the yolk, and the egg white. However, even with these three parts, an egg is still one, just as God is one, even though He exists as three different persons.

  In the same way, water can exist as a liquid, a solid, and as a gas. However, the basic chemical structure of water—two parts hydrogen with one part oxygen—remains the same no matter what form water takes. This is the same with God. Although He appears as the Father, the Son, and the Holy Spirit, He is still one God.

TRIVIA

Which disciple denied knowing Jesus three times?

Peter (John 18:15–18, 25–27).

3 Who Is Jesus? The Lord, Liar, Lunatic Argument

We introduced this chapter by saying that many people try to pass Jesus off as simply a great man, a prophet, or a great moral teacher. But Jesus' claim to be God does not leave us with this option, as C. S. Lewis, author of *Mere Christianity, The Chronicles of Narnia,* and other Christian classics, points out:

> I am trying here to prevent anyone saying the really foolish thing that people often say about Him: "I'm ready to accept Jesus as a great moral teacher, but I don't accept His claim to be God." That is the one thing we must not say. A man who was merely a man and said the sort of things Jesus said would not be a great moral teacher. He would either be a lunatic— on a level with the man who says he is a poached egg—or else he would be the Devil of Hell. You must make your choice. Either this man was, and is, the son of God: or else a madman or something worse.[1]

Lewis's argument in defense of the divinity of Jesus is very difficult to defeat. To help you effectively explain it to your children, let's break it down into three questions:

- *Question: Was Jesus a Liar?*

  Answer: No! If Jesus claimed to be God even though He knew He was not, then He was a liar. And if He was a liar, He was also a hypocrite, because He taught one thing and then did another, and a fool—because His claims to be God led to His crucifixion. But we know Jesus wasn't a liar. How could He have been a great moral teacher, which everyone agrees on, if He lied about something this important? So if Jesus wasn't a liar, what other options are there?

- *Question: Was Jesus a Lunatic?*

  Answer: No! Some people think that if Jesus wasn't purposefully lying about being God, maybe He was just confused. He might have really thought He was God, even though He was just a man. Claiming to be God in the Jewish world of Jesus' time was called blasphemy, and it was punished by death (John 10:33). Someone would have to be crazy or suicidal to make that claim. Take a moment to think about the character of Jesus recorded in the Bible: He was calm, loving, considerate, peaceful, wise—hardly the words you would use to describe a lunatic. And what about His teachings? They are recognized the world over for their wisdom, clarity, and suitability to everyday situations—hardly the ravings of a lunatic. So if Jesus wasn't a liar or a lunatic, what was He?

- *Question: Was Jesus Lord?*

  Answer: Yes! When we look for an answer to the question, "Who is Jesus?" knowing full well that He claimed to be God, we're really left with only one of two options: Either He was telling the truth, and He is God, or His claims are false, and He is not God. We've

TRIVIA

Why did some people want to stone Jesus? *Because He claimed to be God (John 8:56–59).*

[1]C. S. Lewis, *Mere Christianity* (New York: Macmillan, 1952), p.52.

19

disproved the second option by showing that Jesus was neither a liar nor a lunatic. That leaves us with the first option and a choice: to either accept or reject Him as our Savior and Lord.

✞ Prophecy Proves That Jesus Is God

Did you know that Jesus fulfilled sixty major messianic prophecies from the Old Testament? Looking at these prophecies and seeing how they were fulfilled in His life and death is an exciting way to build your children's faith and confirm to them that Jesus really lived. No one can make his or her life fulfill prophecy. For example, we have no choice as to where or when we're born. The only way Jesus could have fulfilled these prophecies was if He really is God.

Prophecies About Jesus

Prophecy	Reference	Fulfillment
• Messiah to be the seed of a woman	Genesis 3:15	Matthew 1:18; Galatians 4:4–5
• Messiah to be the seed of Abraham (a Jew)	Genesis 12:3; 18:18; Isaiah 11:10	Matthew 1:2; Luke 3:34; Acts 3:25; Galatians 3:16
• Messiah to be of the tribe of Judah	Genesis 49:10	Matthew 1:2; Luke 3:34
• Messiah to be of the seed of Jacob and David	Numbers 24:17, 19; Psalm 132:11–12	Matthew 1:2, 6; Luke 1:32–33; 3:34; Romans 1:3
• Messiah to be a prophet like Moses	Deuteronomy 18:15, 19	Matthew 21:11; John 1:45; 6:14; Acts 3:22–23
• Messiah to be the Son of God	Psalm 2:7; Proverbs 30:4	Matthew 3:17; Luke 1:32
• Messiah to be raised from the dead	Psalm 16:10	Acts 13:35–37
• Messiah to be crucified	Psalm 22; 69:21	Matthew 27:34–50; John 19:28–30
• Messiah to be betrayed by a friend	Psalm 41:9	John 13:18, 21, 26–27
• Messiah to ascend to heaven	Psalm 68:18	Luke 24:51; Acts 1:9

JOKE

How many animals did Moses take on the ark?

None. Moses had the Ten Commandments.

Prophecy	Reference	Fulfillment
• Homage and tribute paid to Messiah by great kings	Psalm 72:10–11	Matthew 2:1–11
• Messiah to be a priest like Melchizedek	Psalm 110:4	Hebrews 5:5–6
• Messiah to be at the right hand of God	Psalm 110:1	Hebrews 1:3
• Messiah, the stone the builders rejected, to become the head cornerstone	Psalm 118:22–23; Isaiah 8:14–15; 28:16	Matthew 21:42–43; Acts 4:11; Ephesians 2:20; 1 Peter 2:6–8
• Messiah to be born of a virgin	Isaiah 7:14	Matthew 1:18–25; Luke 1:26–35
• Galilee to be the first area of Messiah's ministry	Isaiah 9:1–8	Matthew 4:12–16
• Messiah will perform miracles	Isaiah 35:5–6	Matthew 11:3–6; John 11:47
• Messiah will minister to the Gentiles	Isaiah 42:1; 49:1–8	Matthew 12:21
• Messiah will be meek and mild	Isaiah 42:2–3; 53:7	Matthew 12:18–20
• Messiah will be beaten	Isaiah 50:6	Matthew 26:67; 27:26, 30
• Messiah's bones will not be broken	Psalm 34:20	John 19:31–37
• Messiah is the Right Arm of God	Isaiah 53:1; 59:16	John 12:38
• Messiah will establish a new and everlasting covenant	Isaiah 55:3–4; Jeremiah 31:31–33	Matthew 26:28; Mark 14:24; Luke 22:20; Hebrews 8:6–13
• Messiah is the Intercessor	Isaiah 59:16	Hebrews 9:15
• The twofold aspect of Messiah's mission	Isaiah 61:1–11	Luke 4:16–21
• The time of Messiah's coming was prophesied	Daniel 9:24–26	Ephesians 1:10

TRIVIA

Which disciple was the first to recognize that Jesus was the Son of God?

Peter (Matthew 16:16).

Prophecy	*Reference*	*Fulfillment*
• Messiah to be born in Bethlehem	Micah 5:2	Matthew 2:1; Luke 2:4–6
• Messiah will enter the temple with authority	Malachi 3:1	Matthew 21:12
• Messiah will enter Jerusalem on a donkey	Zechariah 9:9	Matthew 21:1–10
• Messiah will be pierced	Psalm 22:16; Zechariah 12:10	John 19:34, 37
• Messiah will be forsaken by His disciples	Zechariah 13:7	Matthew 26:31, 56
• The Holy Spirit will come in the days of Messiah	Joel 2:28	Matthew 12:28; John 20:22

The Story of Jesus

Topic

The Greatest Story

Jesus came to earth to save us from our sins. But that's just the bare bones of the story. Who was He really? What did He do? What has He got to do with your children? To answer these questions, we need to fill in the rest of the plot and characters.

The story of Jesus has been called the greatest story ever told. It's the ultimate story of good triumphing over evil—and it's all true! In fact, Jesus' story—a messianic figure from an obscure area rises to become the hero of the people, is eventually defeated by the powers-that-be (because His popularity threatens their authority), then returns in triumph and conquers His enemies in a final glorious battle—is where the "good triumphs over evil" theme in so many stories comes from, including everything from *Ben-Hur* to *The Lion King*. These stories speak strongly to us because they echo the truth of the Gospel that God planted in our hearts. This story of Jesus' triumph over evil is also the best place to find out who God really is and how He wants us to live. Every Christian should read Jesus' story regularly to remind him or herself of God's love and victory.

TRIVIA

Where did Satan tempt Jesus?

In the desert (Matthew 4:1; Mark 1:13; Luke 4:1).

Four Gospels, One Foundation

The fact that the New Testament contains four separate accounts of the life of Jesus is no accident. It not only shows that the followers of Jesus thought it was important to pass on the story of His life for future generations, but it also shows us how important it is to God that we clearly understand the truth about His Son.

The Gospels form the foundation of what the Christian life is about. Each Gospel emphasizes a different aspect of Jesus' life, character, and teachings in order to help us understand Him better. Matthew focuses on His teachings and miracles. Mark is a book of action. He was more concerned with showing us what Jesus did than who He was. The Gospel of Luke gives us one of the most thorough accounts of Jesus' life. He also pays close attention to the individuals whose lives were affected by Jesus. And the Gospel of John emphasizes Jesus' role as the Son of God.

Through the Gospels' descriptions of Jesus, we learn a number of things about God, including His power and authority, as demonstrated by Jesus' power and authority over demons, disease, and nature; His character and how much He loves us, as displayed by Jesus' compassion for the sick and the poor and His love for "sinners"; His plan for us, as explained by Jesus when He talked about how we can have a relationship with God (e.g., John 14:6); and how He wants us to live, as demonstrated by Jesus' life and teachings.

Because the message of the Gospels is the foundation of the Christian life, it is important that you know and understand them and encourage your children to do the same. Help them learn and love the stories of Jesus in all four Gospels so that they will get a complete picture of who He is and what He has done. Then teach them how to live out what they learn so that His teachings will become real in their lives. (For more on this see chapters 6–8.)

Places to Model It!

- Show your children how the life of Jesus demonstrates who God is and how He wants them to live. One way to do this is to constantly refer stories about Jesus back to God. For example, when you read how Jesus had compassion on sick people and healed them, tell your children that He did this to show that God cares about people who are sick.

- Read, and refer to, the story of Jesus on a regular basis. For example, when your children are talking about their favorite stories, take the opportunity to refer to the Gospel story as one of your all-time favorites.

- Demonstrate your enthusiasm and excitement for the Gospels by choosing a favorite Gospel and memorizing passages from it. Recite the passages to your children to show them you consider the Gospels important enough to have committed episodes from the story of Jesus to heart.

Tips to Teach It!

Key Bible Verse:

"Jesus also did many other things. What if every one of them were written down? I suppose that even the whole world would not have room for the books that would be written." (John 21:25)

Key Bible Story:

The story of Jesus did not start or end with the Gospels. It started "in the beginning," when there was only God, and it continues into the present day. In Acts 13:16–39 Paul attempts to put the events of Jesus' life into their proper historical context. Read this story with your children, then discuss the following questions.

- To whom did Paul say the message of salvation had been sent?

- How did God fulfill His promise to the Jewish forefathers?

- Who prophesied that Jesus would rise from the dead? What does this mean for you today?

Teachable Moments

- Choose a video about Jesus (see the Resource List at the back of this book) to rent or own, and watch it on a regular basis as a family. Incorporate a family tradition around this film that includes food, fun, and interaction.

- When you're driving with your family in the car, sitting around a campfire, or doing some other family activity, use the Gospel trivia provided in the Tools to Do It section below (and throughout the book) to test each other's knowledge of the Gospels. It will make a fun family game and a good review.

- Read through *The Chronicles of Narnia* with your children and explain the points in the story that are allegories for Christian truth. For example, when you read about Aslan giving his life as a sacrifice on the stone table in *The Lion, the Witch, and the Wardrobe*, explain that this incident mirrors what Jesus did for us on the cross. (See the Resource List at the back of this book for the titles in the series.)

- When your family is reading a story or watching a movie together, watch for "Christ figures" in the story that parallel the role Jesus played for us. Talk about these characters as a family, specifically about how they are like Jesus and how they are different. Explain how the idea of the "Messiah" or "Savior" originated with Jesus.

Tools to Do It!

1 An "Abridged" Gospel

The following is a shortened account of Jesus' life that you can share with your younger children so they can get the whole story in one reading. Use it as a bedtime story or during your family devotion time.

God gave Mary His own Son as a baby. He chose Joseph to help her look after Him.

Because the baby was God's Son, He was born without sin.

An angel of the Lord appeared to Joseph in a dream. The angel said, "Mary will have a son, and you are to name Him Jesus, for He will save His people from their sins." ("Jesus" means "The Lord saves.")

Just before the baby was born, Joseph and Mary had to go to Bethlehem. While they were there, Mary gave birth to her first child, a son.

God sent angels to tell people about His Son's birth. They came to see this amazing event: God's Son born as a baby!

Jesus grew up just like any other child. He went to school, played with His friends, and obeyed His parents. He was also obedient to His real Father, God. But there was one thing that made Jesus different from every other child: He never sinned!

When Jesus was twelve years old, He was in the temple in Jerusalem discussing deep questions with the Jewish teachers. All who heard Him were amazed at His understanding. Jesus grew both in height and wisdom, and He was loved by God and by all who knew Him.

When Jesus was thirty years old, He started to teach and preach. He taught that God cares about how people think and act. He said, "'You must love the Lord your God with all your heart, all your soul, and all your mind.' This is the first and greatest commandment. A second is equally important: 'Love your neighbor as yourself.'"

Jesus also chose twelve special helpers from among His followers. They were called His "disciples," and He spent much of His time teaching them how God wants us to live.

Jesus told people about God's wonderful plan to bring them back to Himself. He said, "God so loved the world that He gave His only Son, so that everyone who believes in Him will not perish but have eternal life."

When Jesus taught people about God, He used stories (called "parables") to help them understand what He was saying. One story Jesus told was about two men: one foolish man who built his house on the sand and one wise man who built his house on the rock. When the rains came down and the floods came up, the house built on sand came crashing down, but the house built on the rock stood firm. Jesus used this story to show us the difference between obeying Him and going our own way in life. If we obey Jesus, we will stand firm, even when trouble comes. But if we disobey, when trouble comes our lives will fall apart and we won't be able to stand firm.

Jesus also helped people see what God is like. He showed them God loves them. One way He did this was by healing people who were sick, blind, or disabled. Whatever their illness or pain, or if they were possessed

TRIVIA

What did the baby in Elizabeth's womb do when he heard Mary's voice?
He jumped for joy (Luke 1:44).

by demons, or were epileptics, or were paralyzed, Jesus healed them all.

One time a ruler got down on his knees in front of Jesus. He said, "My daughter has just died. But you can come and place your hand on her. Then she will live again." Jesus went and took the girl by the hand, and she stood up!

Jesus did other wonderful and amazing things. He calmed storms and walked on water. Another time, He fed a crowd of more than 5,000 people with only five little barley loaves and two fish!

Jesus showed people that God loves children. He healed them, let them help Him, and even raised them from the dead! Some children were brought to Jesus so He could lay His hands on them and pray for them. The disciples told the parents not to bother Him. When Jesus saw what was happening, He got upset with His disciples and said, "Let the children come to me. Don't stop them!" He took them in His arms and placed His hands on their heads and blessed them.

Not everyone liked Jesus, though. What He did and taught made the religious leaders angry. They were jealous because the people liked Him so much, so they planned to get rid of Him. One night, when Jesus was talking to His friends, the religious leaders sent a crowd with clubs and swords.

The disciples exclaimed, "Lord, should we fight? We brought swords!" And one of them slashed at a servant and cut off his ear.

But Jesus said, "Don't resist anymore." And He touched the place where the man's ear had been and healed him.

Then the crowd grabbed Jesus and arrested Him. They took Him to Pilate, who ruled the area for the Roman government, and put Jesus on trial. The soldiers beat Jesus, put thorns on His head, and made fun of Him. Then Pilate spoke to the people. "I am going to bring Him out to you now, but understand clearly that I find Him not guilty."

But because the leaders spread lies about Jesus and told everyone that He should die, the people yelled, "Away with Him. Crucify Him!"

Then Pilate gave Jesus to them to be crucified, even though He was not guilty of any crime.

They nailed Jesus to the cross.

Jesus said, "Father, forgive these people, because they don't know what they're doing." Two others, both criminals, were executed with Him. One of the criminals said, "Jesus, remember me when you come into your kingdom."

Jesus replied, "I assure you, today you will be with me in paradise."

Later, Jesus cried out to His Father, God, and died.

Jesus' body was put in a tomb by two of His friends. Early on the first day of the week, some women went to the tomb. Suddenly there was a great earthquake, and an angel of the Lord came down from heaven and rolled aside the stone from the tomb doorway.

"Don't be afraid," he said. "I know you are looking for Jesus, who was crucified. He isn't here! He has been raised from the dead, just as he said he would. Now go quickly and tell his disciples."

Later, as the disciples were talking about what had happened, Jesus was suddenly standing there among them. He said, "Peace be with you." But the whole group was terribly frightened. They thought they were seeing a ghost! "Why are you frightened?" He asked. "Look at my hands. Look at my feet. You can see that it's really me. Touch me and make sure that I am not a ghost!"

Jesus was with His disciples for many weeks. He told them to go and tell the world about Him and His teachings. Then, one day when He had finished speaking with the disciples, they watched Him rise into the sky and disappear into a cloud. Two angels told them, "Jesus has been taken away from you into heaven. And someday, just as you saw him go, he will return!"

One day Jesus will come back for all God's children. That's everyone who believes Jesus died for them and has been forgiven. We will be with Him forever.

2 Gospel Reading Plans

Because the story of Jesus is the most important story ever told, the Gospels should be counted as the number one Bible reading priority for your children. Where should they begin? That all depends on their reading ability and where they are in their faith journey. The following are a number of reading plans that your children can use, depending on their age and ability.

- ***Plan 1:*** *The Story of Jesus in an Evening (A Read-with-Me Plan)*

This series of short Bible passages will introduce your children to the main points about who Jesus is, what He taught and did while on earth, and why He died on the cross. This plan is ideal for you to read through in an evening or two with children ages 6–8.

- The Birth of Jesus—Luke 2:4–7
- The Two Greatest Commandments—Matthew 22:34–40
- Jesus the Miracle Worker—Matthew 8:1–9
- The Last Supper—Luke 22:14–23
- Jesus Condemned to Die—Mark 14:55–65
- The Crucifixion—Luke 23:32–34
- Jesus Back from the Dead—Mark 16:1–8
- Jesus Rises into Heaven—Luke 24:50–53

- ***Plan 2:*** *The Story of Jesus in a Week (A Read-on-My-Own Plan)*

Children can use this simple plan to read the main points of the story of Jesus in a week. This plan is ideal for children ages 8–10 who are comfortable reading the Bible on their own but may not be ready to take on an entire Gospel.

MOTTO

Jesus' story is "His-story."

Day One:
> The Birth of Jesus—Luke 2:1–40 or Matthew 2
> Jesus As a Youth—Luke 2:41–52

Day Two:
> The Baptism of Jesus—Matthew 3:13–17
> The Temptation of Jesus—Matthew 4:1–11

Day Three:
> Jesus the Healer—Matthew 8:1–13
> Feeding the Famished—Mark 6:32–44
> Live Twice—John 11:1–3, 17–23, 38–46

Day Four:
> The Two Greatest Commandments—Matthew 22:34–40
> The Good Samaritan—Luke 10:30–37
> The Lost Son—Luke 15:11–32

Day Five:
> The Last Supper—Luke 22:14–23
> Jesus Condemned to Die—Luke 23:13–25

Day Six:
> The Crucifixion—Luke 23:26–56

Day Seven:
> Jesus Returns from the Dead—Luke 24:1–12
> Jesus Rises into Heaven—Luke 24:50–53

- ***Plan 3:*** *The Story of Jesus in a Month (A Read-on-My-Own Plan for Older Children)*

Once your children are ready for a bigger reading challenge, encourage them to choose a Gospel and read through the entire book on their own. Any of the Gospels will serve as a good introduction to Jesus, but some are easier for children to read and understand than others. The following brief descriptions of the Gospels will help your children decide where to begin.

- ***Matthew:*** This Gospel focuses on the teachings and miracles of Jesus. Matthew contains many of the classic teachings of Jesus, including the Sermon on the Mount, the Lord's Prayer, and His parables about the kingdom of God. It also has a number of miracles and the story of the birth of Jesus.

- ***Mark:*** This is a book of action. It focuses more on what Jesus did than on what He said. It is a good place to read about the miracles of Jesus. It is the shortest of all the Gospels.

- ***Luke:*** This Gospel is one of the most complete accounts of the life of Jesus.

- ***John:*** This Gospel most clearly states that Jesus is God. However, John often uses complicated theological language and images that can sometimes be confusing. It may be better to put off reading John until after you have a good handle on the basic points of the

JOKE

Did you hear about the two kids who walked into a church?

It was silly. The second kid should have seen it coming.

story of Jesus presented in the other Gospels.

3 Gospel Trivia

Use the following Gospel trivia questions for a fun review of the Gospel story. They are arranged in three categories: easy, medium, and difficult.

Easy

- Why did Joseph and Mary go to Bethlehem? *Luke 2:1–4*

- What was Jesus' mother's name? *Matthew 1:16*

- In which city was Jesus born? *Matthew 2:1*

- In the parable of the Lost Son, who longed to eat pig food? *Luke 15:16*

- Who betrayed Jesus? *Luke 22:4*

- How did Jesus die? *Luke 24:20*

Medium

- Where did Jesus' parents find Him after losing Him during their journey home from the Passover? *Luke 2:46*

- How old was Jesus when He stayed behind in the temple? *Luke 2:42–43*

- What happened when Jesus rose up out of the water after His baptism? *Matthew 3:16–17*

- What happened to Jesus when He went into the wilderness? *Matthew 4:1*

- What are the two greatest commandments? *Matthew 22:37–39*

- What did Jesus say Peter would do three times before the rooster crowed? *Luke 22:34*

Difficult

- Who was told that he wouldn't die before he saw Christ? *Luke 2:26*

- What was the name of the sea where Jesus met Peter and Andrew? *Matthew 4:18*

- How many basketfuls of bread and fish did the apostles collect after Jesus fed the 5,000? *Mark 6:43*

- During Jesus' trial, who thought Jesus was not guilty? *Matthew 27:19, 24; Luke 23:14–15*

- Who carried Jesus' cross for Him? *Luke 23:26*

- Which disciples ran to the tomb to see if the story the women told about Jesus' resurrection was true? *Luke 24:12*

TRIVIA

Which ruler handed Jesus over to be crucified?
Pilate (Matthew 27:26; Mark 15:15; Luke 23:25; John 19:16).

Jesus Really Lived!

Chapter Four

Topic

Drama in Real Life

Batman! Barney! Mickey Mouse! Children encounter a multitude of fictional characters every day. From books to movies and television to video games, the drama of good against evil is played out again and again by heroes and villains of some author's creation. For this reason, it's important to emphasize to your children that, unlike characters in most other stories, Jesus is real, and the stories about Him are true. Although Jesus left behind no writings or artifacts of His own, the evidence for His existence in both the Bible and in nonbiblical sources is overwhelming.

Let the Bible Speak

The Bible is our main source of information about Jesus. It is the best-preserved ancient manuscript in the world. We have more than 5,000 ancient, handwritten copies or parts of copies of the New Testament, and tens of thousands of copies of the Old Testament. The oldest known portion of a Gospel manuscript contains a few verses of the Gospel of John copied onto a piece of papyrus no more than seventy, and perhaps as little as twenty, years after John first wrote it. The next best-kept ancient document, in terms of how many copies we have and how soon after the original they were made, is a story called *The Iliad* by Homer.

There are only 643 known copies of *The Iliad*, and the oldest was made five hundred years after the original. We also know that the historical events of the Bible are accurate because new archaeological findings continually verify the events and characters recorded in the Bible.

So what does the Bible tell us about Jesus? He was a Jew, with a genealogy that extended all the way back to Abraham (Matthew 1:1–17). He was born of the Virgin Mary; carried out a ministry of healing and teaching; was arrested, tried, and executed by Pontius Pilate; and rose from the dead three days later, after which He appeared several times to His followers before disappearing into the clouds. All of these events are documented in the Gospels, which were written by or based on the writings of Jesus' disciples who witnessed these events firsthand. And His followers all died for what they had seen and believed. Who would die for something he knew was a lie?

Sources Outside of the Bible

The Bible isn't the only historical record that mentions Jesus. His name appears in several non-Christian sources. (See also the Tools to Do It section below.) One example is the writings of Flavius Josephus, a Jewish Pharisee who wrote histories for the Romans around A.D. 70. He confirmed Jesus' existence in this passage:

> Now there was about this time Jesus, a wise man, if it be lawful to call him a man, for he was a doer of wonderful works, a teacher of such men as receive the truth with pleasure. He drew over to him both many of the Jews, and many of the Gentiles. He was [the] Christ, and when Pilate, at the suggestion of the principal men amongst us, had condemned him to the cross, those that loved him at the first did not forsake him, for he appeared to them alive again on the third day as the divine prophets had foretold these and ten thousand other wonderful things concerning him.[1]

The 2,000-year gap between the present and the days when Jesus walked the earth can make Him seem like a myth or a legend to your children, but nothing could be further from the truth. Jesus really lived, and His story is true. The evidence presented in this chapter will help you prove that fact to your children.

Places to Model It!

- The best way to display your belief in the existence of Jesus is to live knowing that He is alive today, and to intentionally model your life and character after His.

- Continually affirm your belief in what the Bible says about Jesus. Constantly refer to His character and teachings when suitable situations arise—for example, when your children are fighting or when you are asked to donate to a person or a cause.

[1]William Whiston, *Josephus: Complete Works* (London: Pickering and Inglis Ltd., 1960), p. 379.

Tips to Teach It!

Key Verse:

"We told you about the time our Lord Jesus Christ came with power. But we didn't make up stories when we told you about it. With our own eyes we saw him in all his majesty." (2 Peter 1:16)

Key Bible Story:

The writers of the Gospels, Jesus' apostles and their assistants, were utterly convinced that what they had seen and experienced was real. These books were based on eyewitness accounts of Jesus' followers. We can be confident that what they say about who Jesus is and what He did is true. Read Luke 1:1–4 with your children and discuss the following questions.

- Why did Luke write his Gospel?

- What evidence did he base his Gospel on?

- Based on this passage, how can you be sure that Jesus really lived?

Teachable Moments

- If you're reading a Bible story about Israel to your children, or if you hear about Israel on the news, get out a map or a globe and show them that Israel is a real place. Talk to them about how many of the cities, towns, and other landmarks (such as Jerusalem and the Sea of Galilee) that existed in Jesus' time still exist today.

- When you're reading a story about Jesus with your children, emphasize that the story is true, that Jesus and the other characters really lived, and that the place where they lived still exists.

- Use a timeline (see Tools to Do It) to show your children how the life of Jesus fits in with other events that were happening around the world while He walked the earth.

- When your children see or talk about make-believe characters as if they are real, explain the difference between real people and make-believe people. Contrast these characters with Jesus, who is real.

JOKE

How do angels greet each other?

They wave halo.

Tools to Do It!

1 More Evidence for Jesus As a Man of History

We mentioned earlier that the Bible provides us with the most reliable information about Jesus. But His name also pops up in documents written by non-Christians during and after Jesus' time. These mentions help to bolster the Bible's claims.

- Cornelius Tacitus (born about A.D. 52), a Roman historian and the governor of Asia, mentions Jesus' death in a document written around A.D. 112. His letter affirms that Jesus, or "Christus," was a real person in history:

    [Nero] falsely charged with the guilt, and punished with the most exquisite tortures, the persons commonly called Christians, who were hated for their enormities. Christus [the Latin word for "Christ"], the founder of the name, was put to death by Pontius Pilate, procurator of Judea in the reign of Tiberius: but the pernicious superstition, repressed for a time broke out again, not only through Judea, where the mischief originated, but through the city of Rome also.[2]

- Josephus, the Jewish historian mentioned earlier, also mentions James the brother of Jesus when he describes the actions of the high priest Ananus. This reference squarely places Jesus in history:

    But the younger Ananus . . . was also of the sect of the Sadducees, who are severe in judgement above all the Jews, as we have already shown. He assembled a council of judges, and brought before it the brother of Jesus the so-called Christ, whose name was James, together with some others, and having accused them as law-breakers, he delivered them over to be stoned.[3]

- The Jewish religious teachers of Jesus' day, called rabbis, also referred to Jesus in their writings. For example:

    On the eve of Passover they hanged Yeshu (of Nazareth) [Yeshu is the Jewish word for Jesus] and the herald went before him for forty days saying (Yeshu of Nazareth) . . . led astray Israel.[4]

[2]Josh McDowell, *Evidence That Demands a Verdict* (San Bernardino: Campus Crusade for Christ, 1972), p. 84.
[3]William Whiston, *Josephus: Complete Works*, p. 423.
[4]Josh McDowell, *Evidence That Demands a Verdict*, p. 88.

Note that although all three of these ancient writers question the truth of Jesus' claim to be God, none of them ever questions that He really lived. Jesus was a real person in history, just like you or me.

- Jesus continued to live even after He died! Take a look at the facts:

1) Jesus Died

- The Romans responsible for Jesus' crucifixion made sure He was dead (John 19:31–35). First they beat Him, and then they nailed Him to a cross. Crucifixion was so brutal that no one could possibly recover from it.

- Jesus was buried in a cave with only one exit, and it was blocked with an enormous stone.

- Jesus' body was wrapped in cloths and spices. The myrrh that was used made the grave clothes stick to the body. They would be difficult to remove.

- Roman soldiers guarded the tomb. They were very careful because if they fell asleep on the job, they would be put to death.

2) A Couple of Days Later . . .

- The tomb was empty. The huge stone had been moved away from the doorway.

- The Roman guards were bribed to say the disciples stole Jesus' body while they slept. But neither they nor the disciples were punished for breaking Roman law.

- The grave clothes were empty, as if Jesus' body had passed through them.

- More than five hundred people said Jesus appeared to them alive after His death.

- The disciples changed from timid people hiding from the authorities to bold people who suffered beatings and death because they believed Jesus rose from the dead.

Read Josh McDowell's book *Evidence That Demands a Verdict* for more proof. Also see the Resource List at the back of this book.

2 The World During Jesus' Time

When you're reading the Gospels, you can get so caught up in the drama and wonder of the story that you forget that, while Jesus ministered in Israel, other important events were going on all around the world. The following is a brief sampling of some of the things that occurred in the world shortly before, during, and after Jesus lived on earth.

TRIVIA

Which prophet predicted that Jesus would be born of a virgin?

Isaiah (Isaiah 7:14).

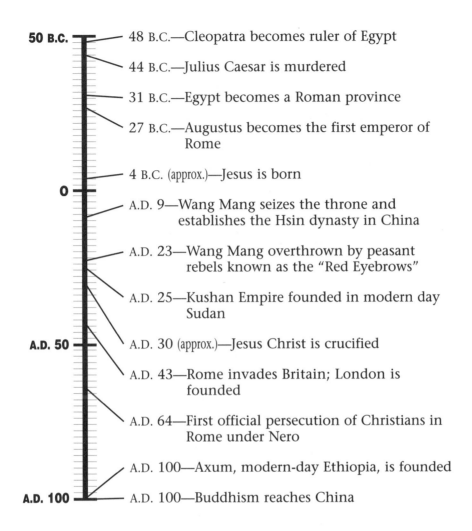

50 B.C. — 48 B.C.—Cleopatra becomes ruler of Egypt

44 B.C.—Julius Caesar is murdered

31 B.C.—Egypt becomes a Roman province

27 B.C.—Augustus becomes the first emperor of Rome

4 B.C. (approx.)—Jesus is born

0 — A.D. 9—Wang Mang seizes the throne and establishes the Hsin dynasty in China

A.D. 23—Wang Mang overthrown by peasant rebels known as the "Red Eyebrows"

A.D. 25—Kushan Empire founded in modern day Sudan

A.D. 50 — A.D. 30 (approx.)—Jesus Christ is crucified

A.D. 43—Rome invades Britain; London is founded

A.D. 64—First official persecution of Christians in Rome under Nero

A.D. 100—Axum, modern-day Ethiopia, is founded

A.D. 100 — A.D. 100—Buddhism reaches China

3 *Anno Domini*—"In the Year of Our Lord"

The arrival of Jesus on earth was such an important event that our entire dating system is divided into two eras: B.C., which stands for "Before Christ," and A.D., which stands for "Anno Domini," a Latin phrase meaning "in the year of our Lord." This dating system was introduced around A.D. 527 by Dionysius Exiguus, a monk who lived in Rome.

Before the establishment of Exiguus's system, the dating system most commonly used in the Roman Empire was measured from the traditional date of the foundation of their city, which was around 753 B.C., or, as the Romans would have said it, 1 A.U.C. (*ab urbe conditâ*, which is Latin for "the founding of the city").

The Romans also marked years by the names of the emperors or rulers then in office. If the emperor had been particularly well liked, the years were often counted according to how many years it had been since the emperor died (i.e., year 3 in the era of Augustus).

This practice of the Romans was the main reason Exiguus decided to develop a new dating system. Exiguus lived in a time period known as the "Era of Diocletian." Diocletian was the emperor of Rome from

TRIVIA

What was Jesus' ethnic background?

Jewish.

TRIVIA

In which city was
Jesus crucified?
Jerusalem.

A.D. 284 to 305. Although he was an able leader, he was no friend of Christians, and Exiguus did not think that the name of a person known for his persecution of Christians should be remembered in this way.

Exiguus decided to fix year 1 of his new dating system at the birth of Jesus, which he calculated took place 753 years from the foundation of Rome (although now scholars think it was 4 years earlier). After receiving approval from the pope, he designated this year 1 of his new era, which he called the years "of our Lord" or Anno Domini. Exiguus's system was adopted gradually, first in Italy, then in other parts of Europe. It came into common use across Europe as a whole shortly after A.D. 1000. The dating system was eventually established and accepted in most countries around the world, though some, such as Israel and many Muslim countries, still do not use this dating system today. They have their own calendars based on their own religions.

The Message of Salvation

Topic

Since the Beginning of Time

Have you heard the Good News? Have your children? It's the heart of Jesus' story and the reason we can be so glad that His story is true. From the moment God created Adam and Eve, His desire has been to have a loving relationship with you and your children. But God did not demand that relationship. Instead, He gave Adam and Eve, and all people, the choice either to accept His love or reject it. He wants everyone to love Him freely. But Adam and Eve rejected Him. This is called "sin," and the punishment was separation from God and death. Everyone born since Adam and Eve is sinful and separated from God, too. But don't worry. God had a solution in mind right from the beginning.

The Perfect Sacrifice

Apart from Jesus, there is no way for anyone to cross the barrier of sin that separates us from God. In Old Testament times, the Israelites offered sacrifices, as God's Law required, to take away their sins. But even these sacrifices were not enough, because they had to keep offering them year after year.

Jesus was sacrificed once and for all, for everyone. He was conceived of the Holy Spirit and born of a virgin. The Virgin Birth is important because it means that Jesus was not just a man who claimed to be God. He was God. Also, because He was fathered by the Holy Spirit, who is holy and sinless, Jesus was born innocent, perfect, and without sin. As the new sacrifice, Jesus paid the penalty for our sins so that we could all be forgiven and become God's children once again. All we need to do is confess our sins, trust in Jesus as our Savior, and accept God's forgiveness and authority in our lives.

Leading Your Child to Jesus

Many parents wonder how and when to lead their children to Jesus. Relax. Becoming a Christian is not like signing a legal document; it's initiating a relationship. This implies three things: One, the nature of the relationship will vary from person to person, just as your relationship with your children varies from child to child. Two, the proper time for this relationship to begin will also vary. Three, the way each person comes to Christ will be different. Some children will become Christians through Sunday school, some at summer camp, some through their parents, some on their own through prayer, and so on.

No matter what your child's unique bent, you can play a part in leading him or her to Jesus by sharing the Gospel story with him or her and creating opportunities to talk about Jesus and how to start a relationship with Him. Remember, God wants your children to come to Him even more than you do. He's working with them and will help them to trust Jesus as Savior. There's no need to push. Just tell the story and show your children what a wonderful opportunity they have to know Jesus.

MOTTO

Jesus died for me;
now I live for Him.

Places to Model It!

- One of the best ways to get your children interested in following Jesus is to share your own testimony with them. They will be excited to learn how God worked in your life. Get other family members or friends to share their testimonies from time to time. (Note: When giving your testimony, don't glamorize any sinful habits or lifestyles you may have participated in before you became a Christian. This will distract children from the point of your testimony, which is to tell how your relationship with Jesus has transformed your life.)

- Show your children that your life has been changed by Jesus. You can also explain that you do certain things, such as donating to the poor or volunteering at the church or hospital or responding to others with love and kindness because Jesus called you to love others as He loves you.

- Use the parent-child relationship you have with your children as an example of how their relationship with God works. For example, you tell them to do things because you love them and want what's best for them. They obey you because they trust you. Things should work the same way in their relationship with God.

Tips to Teach It!

Key Bible Verse:

> *"God loved the world so much that he gave his one and only Son. Anyone who believes in him will not die but will have eternal life."* (John 3:16)

Key Bible Story:

Jesus' late night conversation with Nicodemus the Pharisee tells us a lot about salvation and what we need to do to be saved. Read John 3:1–21 with your children, then discuss the following questions. (When you have finished reading John, read Paul's explanation of how to accept Jesus in Romans 10:9–10.)

- How did Nicodemus know Jesus came from God?

- Why did God send His one and only Son into the world?

- What do we need to do to be saved?

Teachable Moments

- When you're reading the story of Jesus with your children or watching it on film, use the opportunity to tell them about what Jesus has done for them.

- When you're talking about Jesus' story, contextualize it by explaining how God's plan for salvation was created before the beginning of the world to solve a problem that goes back to the sin of Adam and Eve.

- Use life opportunities as they come up to relate back to the message of Jesus. For example, when your children feel guilty about something they have done, talk about forgiveness and how Jesus paid the penalty for their sins. All your children have to do is pray and ask for forgiveness. Because of Jesus, God will forgive them (Romans 10:13). (See the model prayer on the next page.)

- When your children hear something bad on the news, talk to them about the effects of sin on our world. Also remind them that no matter how bad things may seem now because of sin, God is in control, and His plan will win out over sin and its effects.

TRIVIA

What was Adam and Eve's sin in the Garden of Eden? *They disobeyed God by eating the forbidden fruit (Genesis 3).*

Tools to Do It!

1 A Salvation Prayer

When your children decide to accept Jesus as their Savior and Master, have them pray the following simple prayer or use it as a model for their own prayer.

Dear God, I know I'm a sinner. I've made wrong choices and done bad things. I'm sorry. Please forgive me. I know Your Son, Jesus, died for my sins, and I believe You raised Him from the dead. I want Jesus as my Lord and Master. Thank You for loving me and making me Your child. Now, please fill me with Your Holy Spirit, so I'll have the strength I need to obey You. In Jesus' name, amen.

2 Questions Children Ask About Salvation

The following are questions commonly asked about salvation by children, followed by "kid friendly" answers that you can read directly to your children or use as a basis for your response.

- *Question:* Why do God and Jesus love people?

  Answer: God loves us because He is God, and He created us, not because we're good or nice people. In fact, no one could ever be good enough to be worthy of God's love. Just like a parent, God loves you no matter what. Isn't that great?

  Key Verses: John 1:12; Romans 5:8

- *Question:* How can Jesus fit in my heart?

  Answer: When we say "Jesus is in my heart," we don't mean our physical heart. We just mean deep down inside, where you really feel and believe. It means that you have asked Jesus to be your Savior—to forgive and take care of you and to be in charge of your life. When you ask Jesus to take over, God really does come inside—the Holy Spirit comes and lives inside you. And the Holy Spirit can be in all of the people who love God at the same time. Jesus wants to be very close to you, too, like a good friend. Through His Holy Spirit, He wants to "live in your heart."

  Key Verses: John 16:7–8; Colossians 1:26–27

TRIVIA

What is the penalty for sin?
Death (Romans 6:23).

- *Question:* How do you get Jesus in your heart?

  Answer: You become a Christian by asking Jesus to forgive you and take over your life. You know that you have done wrong things, that you have sinned, and you recognize that you need Jesus to forgive your sins. So you tell Him about your sins and ask for His forgiveness. Then you listen to Him and obey what He tells you to do.

  Key Verses: John 5:24; Acts 19:18; Romans 3:21–24

- *Question:* Why isn't everyone a Christian?

  Answer: There are two main reasons why not everyone is a Christian: One, not everyone has heard about Jesus, so there is no way yet for them to become Christians. That is why we need to go out and tell the good news about what Jesus has done for us. Two, not everyone wants to be a Christian, even after they have heard the good news. God doesn't force people to follow Jesus. Some people not only reject Jesus, but they are mean to people who follow Him. That's because they don't understand the love that God has for them. You should also try to tell these people about God's love for them.

  Key Verses: Matthew 7:14; John 15:9; 17:13–16

3 *Additional Verses About Salvation*

The following verses may help you explain the concept and meaning of salvation to your children. (See also the verses in the Tools to Do It section of chapter 11.)

- *"My sheep listen to my voice. I know them, and they follow me. I give them eternal life, and they will never die. No one can steal them out of my hand."* (John 10:27–28)

- *"I am not ashamed of the good news. It is God's power. And it will save everyone who believes."* (Romans 1:16)

- *"One man sinned [Adam], and death ruled because of his sin. But we are even more sure of what will happen because of what the one man, Jesus Christ, has done. Those who receive the rich supply of God's grace will rule with Christ in his kingdom. They have received God's gift and have been made right with him."* (Romans 5:17)

- *"Scripture says, 'Everyone who calls on the name of the Lord will be saved.'"* (Romans 10:13)

- *"God didn't choose us to receive his anger. He chose us to receive salvation because of what our Lord Jesus Christ has done. Jesus died for us. Some will be alive when he comes. Others will be dead. Either way, we will live together with him. So cheer each other up with the hope that you have. Build each other up. In fact, that's what you are doing."* (1 Thessalonians 5:9–11)

The Teachings of Jesus

Topic

The Master Teacher

Knowing Jesus as Savior is the beginning of a new life for your children. Jesus introduces them to this new life and teaches them how to live it.

Jesus Christ is recognized the world over as one of the greatest teachers who ever lived. Even people who don't believe that He is the Son of God acknowledge that what He taught and how He taught it are unmatched in the history of the world.

Throughout His ministry, Jesus taught about a number of topics— love, life, death, hell, healing, marriage—but He didn't approach the topics by teaching long, confusing doctrines or philosophies. Instead, His teachings were practical and to the point. They focused on how we should live, the character we should develop, and how we should behave toward God and others. For example, He told us that our prayers didn't have to be long, showy, and complicated. Instead, He gave us a simple model called "The Lord's Prayer," which we can pray on our own from our hearts (Matthew 6:9–13). He told us not to think we could please God if we were not getting along with other people (Matthew 5:23–24). He also said we should take care of our own faults instead of criticizing others (Luke 6:41–42).

In fact, Jesus summed up His teachings in two simple commands: *"Love the Lord your God with all your heart and with all your soul. Love him with all your mind,"* and *"love your neighbor as you love yourself"* (Matthew 22:37–40). If we live by these commands, we will be living the life God planned for us.

Becoming Like Jesus

Jesus' followers called Him "rabbi" (Mark 9:5; John 1:38), which is a Jewish word for "teacher." Young Jewish men in Jesus' time who wanted to study the Scriptures (the Old Testament) would choose a rabbi and become his disciple. They would listen to and memorize his teachings. They would also watch their teacher's life and try to live as he did. When the rabbi decided a student was ready, he would make him a teacher so that he could have his own disciples. By then, the student would think and live just like his teacher.

Jesus used this teaching method with His disciples. He taught that the way to live was to follow His example. In fact, the word "Christian" means "little Christ" or "Christlike." What kind of example did He set for us? He showed us how to be loving, kind, forgiving, merciful, gentle, humble, patient, compassionate. In other words, He showed us how to be like God.

WWJD?

Following Jesus' example is the ultimate way to live. He created life, and He knows how it works best, so following Him leads to the best possible life. If your children have any doubts about how to deal with certain situations, teach them to stop and ask themselves, "What would Jesus do?" ("WWJD?" for short). For example, when they are tempted to gossip about someone at school, they can think of what Jesus would do in the same situation. By stopping to ask themselves, "WWJD?" they will remember that Jesus loved everyone. He would never do or say anything that would hurt another person. If your children love and obey Jesus, they will follow His example.

An entire movement has grown up around the concept of *WWJD?* complete with books, games, web sites, and jewelry that will help children remember this important question (see the Resource List at the back of this book). Using this question with them is an effective way to teach children how to live their new life by patterning their lives after Jesus and making His character their own.

Places to Model It!

- The most powerful way to teach your children who Jesus is and how He wants them to live is to obey His teachings yourself. Let your children see you ask what Jesus would do in certain situations and then act accordingly. For example, if you realize that the grocery clerk gave you too much change, ask yourself out loud, "What would Jesus do?" Then return the money. This may feel a little ridiculous at first, but you need to be intentional with your children about explaining why you behave the way you do.

- Show them that Jesus' two commands—love God and love others— are the two greatest priorities in your life. You can do this by constantly placing every decision and situation before God and by acknowledging the importance of the needs and desires of others. For example, if you're tired and just want to relax for the evening but your spouse asks you to do a chore, put aside your own agenda and display a servant attitude by helping out.

- Many people pick and choose which of Jesus' teachings they will obey and which they will disregard. Instead, make every effort to demonstrate, through word and deed, that you accept, respect, and try to obey all of Jesus' teachings in every situation. For example, you should model to your children that you should always tell the truth, not only when it benefits you, but even if it means you'll get in trouble.

Tips to Teach It!

Key Bible Verse:

"Jesus finished saying all these things. The crowds were amazed at his teaching. He taught like one who had authority. He did not speak like their teachers of the law." (Matthew 7:28–29)

Key Bible Story:

As you will read in this story, from the moment Jesus first got up to teach in the temple, the people recognized something special about the way He taught. They were also amazed that someone could be so wise without having gone to a special school. Read John 7:14–29 with your children, then discuss the following questions.

- Why were the Jews amazed at Jesus' teaching?
- What did Jesus claim was the secret to His teaching?
- Why should we obey Jesus' teachings?

Teachable Moments

- The most important place to teach children how to love God and others is at home. Relationships with parents, siblings, and friends are the training ground for successful relationships later on in life. You're helping them obey Jesus' teachings by helping them learn to get along with their brothers and sisters. Tell them that doing things God's way is always the best way. When they choose to love and forgive and cooperate, they learn more about getting along. The more they know how to get along with others, the more friends they'll have, and the happier their lives will be.

• When your children are angry at one of their friends and don't want to forgive, or if they keep teasing and criticizing each other, encourage them to ask themselves, "What would Jesus do?" and then work through the situation with them from Jesus' perspective. Do this with them until thinking like Jesus becomes second nature.

Tools to Do It!

1 The Classic Teachings of Jesus

Jesus taught on a wide variety of topics, including everything from money to marriage. The following is a list of some of His "classic" teachings—timeless teachings that His followers have treasured throughout the centuries. Read through and discuss these with your children. If you can, memorize the passages or portions of the passages with your children so that the words of Jesus will never be far from their hearts.

- *The Beatitudes*—Matthew 5:3–12; Luke 6:20–26
- *Salt and Light*—Matthew 5:13–16
- *Turn the Other Cheek*—Matthew 5:38–42
- *Give to the Needy*—Matthew 6:1–4
- *How to Pray*—Matthew 6:5–15; Luke 11:2–4
- *Treasure in Heaven*—Matthew 6:19–24
- *Don't Worry*—Matthew 6:25–34
- *Don't Judge Others*—Matthew 7:1–6; Luke 6:37–42
- *Ask, Seek, Knock*—Matthew 7:7–12
- *The Narrow and Wide Gates*—Matthew 7:13–14
- *A Tree and Its Fruit*—Matthew 7:15–23; Luke 6:43–44
- *Two Sparrows*—Matthew 10:29–31
- *The Cost of Discipleship*—Matthew 10:37–39; Mark 8:34–38; Luke 14:25–35
- *Clean and Unclean*—Matthew 15:10–20; Mark 7:18–23
- *Don't Cause Children to Sin*—Matthew 18:2–9; Mark 9:42–50
- *The Two Greatest Commandments*—Matthew 22:35–40
- *The Last Shall Be First*—Mark 10:29–31, 42–45
- *Have Faith*—Mark 11:22–26; Luke 17:6
- *Watch and Pray*—Mark 13:32–37
- *Love Your Enemies*—Luke 6:27–36

TRIVIA

What's another name for the Beatitudes?
The Blessings.

TRIVIA

What does the Jewish word "rabbi" mean?
Teacher.

- *A Lamp on a Stand*—Luke 8:16–18
- *With God, All Things Are Possible*—Luke 18:24–27
- *God Sent His Son into the World*—John 3:16–18
- *Jesus Is the Resurrection and the Life*—John 11:25–26
- *God's House Has Many Rooms*—John 14:2–4
- *Jesus Is the Only Way to God*—John 14:6

2 WWJD?

The following are a number of ethical situations that you can discuss with your children to help them think like Jesus. Present the situation, then ask, "What would Jesus do?" If your children need help answering, have them refer to the Bible reference provided. Not all the references are to the Gospels. That's because all the life principles taught in the Bible are what Jesus would do. He inspired them all and lived them out while He was on earth.

- *Situation:* Your friend wants to tell you an inappropriate story during recess. WWJD?

  Key Bible verse: "*Finally, my brothers and sisters, always think about what is true. Think about what is noble, right and pure. Think about what is lovely and worthy of respect. If anything is excellent or worthy of praise, think about those kinds of things.*" (Philippians 4:8)

  Lesson: Keep yourself holy and pure, just like Jesus.

- *Situation:* You get to your car after buying your new Turbo-Soaker water gun and realize the clerk gave you too much change. WWJD?

  Key Bible verse: "*Do not steal.*" (Mark 10:19)

  Lesson: Be honest and truthful, just as Jesus taught.

- *Situation:* One of the girls in your class hardly ever has anything to eat at lunchtime. Your mom always packs you a big, tasty lunch. WWJD?

  Key Bible verse: "*Suppose someone gives even a cup of cold water to a little one who follows me. What I'm about to tell you is true. That one will certainly be rewarded.*" (Matthew 10:42)

  Lesson: Give to others because God has given to you.

- *Situation:* Your parents tell you to get your chores done before you go out and play, but they won't be home for an hour. WWJD?

  Key Bible verse: "*Honor your father and mother.*" (Matthew 19:19)

  Lesson: Honor and obey your parents because God put them in authority over you and they do everything they can to love and care for you.

- *Situation:* The children in your class are all picking on an unpopular child. WWJD?

TRIVIA

What did Jesus say were the two greatest commands?

To love God and to love others (Matthew 22:37–40).

Key Bible verse: "*Love your neighbor as you love yourself.*" (Matthew 22:39)

Lesson: God created everyone in His image, so everyone deserves to be treated well.

- *Situation:* You accidentally kick your friend's soccer ball into the street, and it gets run over by a truck. He gets angry and starts yelling at you. WWJD?

Key Bible verse: "*A gentle answer turns anger away. But mean words stir up anger.*" (Proverbs 15:1)

Lesson: Don't lose your temper just because someone else loses his.

- *Situation:* You've just finished building a beautiful sand castle on the beach when a girl runs by and stomps all over it. You notice she has a beautiful sand castle of her own just a few feet away. WWJD?

Key Bible verse: "*Suppose someone hits you on one cheek. Turn your other cheek to him also.*" (Luke 6:29)

Lesson: When someone does something bad to you, you shouldn't do the same back to him. Two wrongs don't make a right. Forgive him instead.

- *Situation:* Everyone is saying bad things about a boy at school. He did do something wrong, and he's really sorry about it. But now none of your friends will talk to him or hang out with him. WWJD?

Key Bible verse: "*You look at the bit of sawdust in your friend's eye. But you pay no attention to the piece of wood in your own eye. Hou can you say to your friend, 'Let me take the bit of sawdust out of your eye'? How can you say this while there is a piece of wood in your own eye? You pretender! First take the piece of wood out of your own eye. Then you will be able to see clearly to take the bit of sawdust out of your friend's eye.*" (Matthew 7:3–5)

Lesson: Don't judge others unless your your own life is in order.

*Note: There are many excellent WWJD? books, games, and other specialty items that you may be interested in purchasing for your children. Consult the Resource List or look for them on the Internet or at your local Christian bookstore.

TRIVIA

Who didn't believe in the resurrection of God's people, the Pharisees or the Sadducees? *The Sadducees. That's why they were very "Sad-you-see."*

3 *You, Then Us, Then Me*

Another useful tool to help your children model their behavior after Jesus is the "You, then us, then me" philosophy. It's simple: Whenever you're in a situation when things aren't going your way, first consider the needs and desires of the other person(s) involved ("You"). Then come up with a solution that benefits everyone involved ("Us"). Only then should you look at a solution that benefits yourself ("Me"). If you put this model into practice, you'll find that you rarely have to worry about your own needs. God's way always works. When you put others first, God takes care of you.

4 *The Two Greatest Commands*

> "Love the Lord your God with all your heart and with all your soul. Love him with all your mind. Love your neighbor as you love yourself."

MOTTO

I always do what Jesus would do.

The Parables of Jesus

Chapter Seven

Topic

He Spoke in Parables

Everyone loves a story. Stories are one of the most effective ways to communicate our deepest feelings and experiences. Few people, including your children, will remember the points from a complex theological lecture on love and forgiveness, but few people forget *The Lion, the Witch, and the Wardrobe* and its message of redemption, love, and forgiveness. The power of story goes straight to the core of who we are as humans.

Jesus knows that people love stories, and He used them to make His teachings memorable and exciting, to bring them to life in the minds of His listeners. He related tales about rebellious sons, lost treasures, wise and foolish managers, beggars, rich men—even weeds. But He didn't tell the stories just for fun. All of Jesus' stories, called *parables,* had an underlying meaning that helped clarify or explain what He was teaching.

A parable is a short, simple story designed to communicate a spiritual truth, principle, or moral lesson. Jesus used parables to illustrate truth by using something people could understand, such as seeds or sheep, to explain something that they didn't understand, such as the kingdom of God. For example, He taught people that they had to give up everything and follow Him if they hoped to enter the kingdom of God. But He needed to show them how important the kingdom of God is compared to the things of this world. He did this by telling a series of stories that compared the kingdom of God to priceless treasures on earth—first a treasure hidden in a field (Matthew 13:44), then a fine pearl (Matthew 13:45–46). This made the kingdom of heaven tangible for people and showed them it was worth sacrificing everything for.

Sharing Jesus' Parables with Your Children

Adults love stories, but children love them even more. Sharing the parables of Jesus with your children is one of the most effective ways to get them interested in learning more about God and His Word. Think back to your own childhood. If you attended Sunday school, vacation Bible school, or Bible camp, you likely sat through many lessons about God, the Bible, and Jesus. But what do you remember? You may recall some of the things your teachers told you about love, forgiveness, and so on. But probably what really stuck with you was a handful of stories such as the Good Samaritan, Noah and the ark, Moses and the Israelites crossing the Red Sea, and so on. You may not have grasped the full implications of the stories right away, but you still enjoyed and remembered them until the time came when you were old enough to understand their true meanings.

Sharing Jesus' parables is a "painless" way to pass on spiritual truths to your children. You can tell the stories and let them stand on their own, or you can do what Jesus did and use them as leaping-off points for discussions about God, heaven, and how we should treat others. Your children may not always appreciate a rebuke or a lesson, but they will always appreciate a good story. Use the stories of Jesus to help them grow in their relationship with God.

Places to Model It!

- As parents, you can tell your children the parables of Jesus. But you can also draw effective, dramatic, parables from your own life. Do this by telling how God's truth was lived out in your life or became clear in a particular situation. For example, perhaps there was a time when you had to give up something in order to help someone, and you ended up receiving something better than what you sacrificed.

- When you see one of Jesus' parables playing itself out in your life, bring it to your children's attention. For example, have you seen someone who was selfish end up learning to love? Do you, or your children, receive God's forgiveness when you feel you "don't deserve it"? What have you put aside to seek God's kingdom? Tell them the parable the situation reminds you of, then tell how you followed the principle taught and how it turned out.

Tips to Teach It!

Key Bible Verse:

"Jesus spoke all these things to the crowd in parables; he did not say anything to them without using a parable. So was fulfilled what was spoken through the prophet: 'I will open my mouth in parables, I will utter things hidden since the creation of the world.'" **(Matthew 13:34–35)**

Key Bible Story:

One of Jesus' most famous parables is the Good Samaritan (Luke 10:30–37). This story teaches us that we are to love and help everyone, no matter who they are or how we feel about them. Read this parable with your children and discuss the following questions.

- Why do you think the priest and the Levite didn't help the wounded man?

- How do you think the wounded man felt when the first two men passed him by? What about when the Samaritan helped him?

- What can you learn from this story about how to treat others?

Teachable Moments

- When you're reading Jesus' parables to your children, encourage them to come up with their own stories that teach a simple life lesson. This can also be done when the family is out on a walk or doing some other activity. A fun way to do this is to have the children name a common object, two names, and a situation, and then come up with a story that uses them to teach a moral lesson. (An example of how to do this is in the Tools to Do It section below.)

- If you are discussing with your children a situation that relates to one of Jesus' parables, talk about the parable and how it helps you deal wisely with the situation. If your child is complaining about having to do chores around the house, share the parable of the talents (Matthew 25:14–30), which teaches that before people can be trusted with big things, they first have to show themselves trustworthy with little things. Children will respond much more positively to correction when it is presented in this form.

- With a dash of elaboration and a little bit of flair, you can turn any one of Jesus' parables into an intriguing bedtime story. (For tips on how to do this, see Tools to Do It.)

Tools to Do It!

1 *The Parables of Jesus*

The following is a list of the parables of Jesus, including one lesson we can learn from each and where they can be found in the Gospels.

- **The Sower**

  Where found: Matthew 13:5–8; Mark 4:3–8; Luke 8:5–8

  Lesson: We need to listen to, learn, and actively apply Jesus' teachings in our lives without getting distracted or tempted by other things.

- **The Weeds**

  Where found: Matthew 13:24–30

  Lesson: We will be rewarded for loving God and following Jesus' teachings when He returns to the earth.

- **The Mustard Seed**

  Where found: Matthew 13:31–32; Mark 4:31–32; Luke 13:19

  Lesson: When we first learn to follow God and He starts working in our hearts and lives, it may seem difficult. But if we persist, God's kingdom—His character and way of doing things—will take over our lives and become natural for us.

- **The Hidden Treasure and the Pearl of Great Price**

  Where found: Matthew 13:44–46

  Lesson: The kingdom of heaven is worth giving up everything for, because God's way is the best way. He knows how everything works. When we seek God and follow Jesus, we find the keys to life's true treasures.

- **The Unmerciful Servant**

  Where found: Matthew 18:23–35

  Lesson: God has forgiven us so we should forgive others. If we don't forgive others, God won't forgive us.

- **The Workers in the Vineyard**

  Where found: Matthew 20:1–16

  Lesson: God rewards us as He wants, according to our willingness to serve Him. We shouldn't compare ourselves to others but do our best with God's help to keep learning and growing.

- **The Two Sons**

  Where found: Matthew 21:28–32

  Lesson: It's not enough to say we will obey God; we have to do it.

- **The Wicked Landowner**

  Where found: Matthew 21:33–46; Mark 12:1–12; Luke 20:9–19

  Lesson: Jesus told this parable to the Jews, who were neither seeking nor obeying God. They even rejected God's Son. Today, this parable teaches us that God made and owns everything and, as Christians, we need to continue to seek and obey God in everything.

- **The Ten Virgins**

  Where found: Matthew 25:1–13

  Lesson: We need to go to God every day, desiring to know Him more and to be more like Jesus, and trusting Him to help us and change us. Thinking our Christian faith is something we can just believe and let sit on the back burner until we need something or get in trouble is like expecting a flashlight to work even though we don't change the dead batteries.

- **The Talents**

  Where found: Matthew 25:14–30

  Lesson: Make the most of what God has given you. Do everything you do with all your heart and ability, and He will give you more.

- **The Seed Growing Secretly**

  Where found: Mark 4:26–29

  Lesson: As you read God's Word, learn more about Him and His ways, and choose to follow His Word, it will be like a seed growing inside of you, filling your heart and mind. When this seed is full grown, the rewards are great.

- **The Two Debtors**

  Where found: Luke 7:41–43

  Lesson: No matter how big or small your mistakes or sins, God is able to forgive them and help you grow. But remember, you please God by trusting Him to help you live His way, not by trying to do things on your own. So, whether your sins are big or little, it's still God's kindness that forgives you and helps you learn.

- **The Good Samaritan**

  Where found: Luke 10:25–37

TRIVIA

What two things did Jesus use in His parables to describe the value of the kingdom of heaven?

A treasure hidden in a field and a precious pearl (Matthew 13:44–46).

Lesson: Strive to do good to everyone, no matter who they are.

- **The Rich Fool**

Where found: Luke 12:16–21

Lesson: Don't store up treasures for yourself on earth. Instead, be rich toward God.

- **The Barren Fig Tree**

Where found: Luke 13:6–9

Lesson: God is patient with you. He is always willing to help you and give you a chance to learn and grow.

- **The Great Supper**

Where found: Luke 14:16–24

Lesson: Those who refuse God's invitation will not be allowed into His kingdom.

- **The Lost Sheep and The Lost Piece of Money**

Where found: Matthew 18:12–14; Luke 15:8–10

Lesson: God wants everyone to be saved. He actively goes after people who don't know Him. Then He celebrates over every person who decides to follow Him.

- **The Prodigal Son**

Where found: Luke 15:11–32

Lesson: God lets us choose how we want to live our lives. But following His way always works best.

- **The Rich Man and Lazarus**

Where found: Luke 16:19–31

Lesson: Obey God in this life because you won't get a second chance after you die.

- **The Friend at Midnight and the Persistent Widow**

Where found: Luke 11:5–8; 18:1–8

Lesson: If you need something, be persistent in your prayers and keep trusting God for it.

- **The Pharisee and the Tax Collector**

Where found: Luke 18:10–14

Lesson: Relying on your own righteousness and performance doesn't get you anywhere with God. But when you confess your sins and rely on God's mercy and help, He will respond. This not only applies when you receive salvation, but every day as you rely on God rather than your own strength and wisdom.

- **The Three Servants**

Where found: Luke 19:12–27

TRIVIA

In which parable do some foolish women run out of lamp oil before a wedding banquet? *The parable of the Ten Virgins (Matthew 25:1–13).*

Lesson: To everyone who is faithful with what he has, more will be given. But those who are unfaithful, even the little bit they have will be taken away.

- **Other Parables**

  - The Leaven—Matthew 13:33; Luke 13:21

  - The Net—Matthew 13:47–50

  - The Marriage of the King's Son—Matthew 22:1–4

  - The Shrewd Manager—Luke 16:1–9

  - The Unprofitable Servants—Luke 17:7–10

2 *Turning Parables into Bedtime Stories*

With a bit of imagination, the parables of Jesus can be turned into interesting, dramatic bedtime stories that will teach your children valuable lessons. All that's needed is to add a bit of flavor and color to make the stories more immediate and relevant to them today. Don't be afraid to make the stories fun. It will make them more interesting. Here are some things you can do:

- Add fun details, such as where the people lived, what they ate for dinner, and so on. You can do this because the parables are just stories and adding such details won't take away from the truths that they teach.

- Modernize the parables. Transport them into modern settings. For example, instead of a simple house on rock and a house on sand, make them into a beautiful mansion on a cliff overlooking the ocean, and a sprawling beach house on the seashore.

- Take the principal points from the story and invent a new story that teaches the same lesson.

3 *Fun Family Parables*

You and your children can come up with your own parables based on a name, a situation, and a commonplace object. This is a fun exercise that you can do at home, in the car, or on a family outing.

This method of storytelling is particularly effective if you want to teach your children a life lesson in a nonthreatening way. For example, you gave your children money and asked them to spend it wisely, but instead they spent it on junk food and video games. Get them to name an object, a character, and a situation. Trust God and start telling the story. After the story, ask a couple of questions to help your children think about the lesson you wanted to teach. Here is a sample story to show you how it works.

Object: Toaster

Character: A parrot named Ike

Situation: At the breakfast table

Lesson: When we follow good advice, things turn out well. But when we ignore it and do things our own way, we can get into trouble.

Ike the parrot wanted breakfast, but not any old breakfast would do. He liked crackers—yes, he knew that was really typical for a parrot—but there was only one way he liked to eat them: slightly toasted, with just a hint of butter on top.

Now that was fine and dandy when Susan and Bill, his owners, were around. They would toast the crackers for Ike and dab them with butter, just the way he liked them. Susan and Bill had even taught him how to push down the toaster handle and say, "Squawk! The toast has popped," when the crackers were done.

But today, Susan and Bill did not wake up at their usual time. Ike waited patiently on his perch for more than an hour, but there was still no sign of them. He tried a few "Good morning" squawks, but even that didn't work. Now he was getting desperate; he wanted crackers!

Ike eyed the toaster where it sat on the counter. It was plugged in, and a box of crackers and a dish of butter sat beside it. *Maybe if I take just one*, he thought. Then Ike remembered what Bill had told him when he first showed him how to push the toaster handle down: "Ike, you must never, ever, try and pull the crackers out on your own. You'll burn your beak, and then you'll be in a heap of trouble." But even as he thought about Bill's words, Ike was slowly hopping toward the toaster.

"What's the harm in one little cracker?" he said to himself. "I can pull a cracker out of a toaster without hurting myself."

Ike snatched a cracker out of the box with his beak, dropped it into the toaster, and pushed down the handle. Now all he had to do was wait. And wait. But something was wrong. His crackers never took this long.

Ike peeked inside the toaster. Oh, no! The cracker was turning dark brown, and the edges were going black. He had to find a way to stop the toaster before it ruined his cracker. Ike looked around for help. He tried one more "Squawk" in hopes of rousing Susan and Bill, but no one appeared.

Ike decided he had to do something. He leaped up onto the toaster, plunged his beak inside, and grabbed hold of the cracker. But something didn't feel right. And what was that awful burned smell? Suddenly Ike leaped back as he realized that smell was coming from his beak!

Ike fell off the counter and onto the floor, and the toaster went flying. In a moment, Bill and Susan were at the door to see what all the racket was about. Then they saw Ike, lying dazed on the floor with a smoldering black

RIDDLE

I was once so hungry that I ate pig food. Who am I?

The lost son from Jesus' parable (Luke 15:11–32).

lump where the tip of his beak used to be. Bill bent down to help Ike to his feet.

"Ike, what did I tell you about not taking the crackers out of the toaster? You should have listened to me. Now we're going to have to clip and bandage your beak until it gets better. There'll be no more crackers for you for a while."

Ike groaned at the thought of no more crackers, but he was thankful to still have most of his beak left. And he had learned a valuable lesson that he would never forget for the rest of his life.

Now ask your children a couple of questions to start a discussion. For example, "What was Ike's first mistake?"

The Miracles of Jesus

Topic

Power Without Limit

"It's a miracle!" How often have you used those words without thinking about what they really mean? We live in an age where "miracles" seem to happen every day. Achievements in the fields of technology and medicine that were the stuff of fantasy a few decades ago are now realities that we take for granted. Space flight is almost routine, communication has reached the point where we can observe any event anywhere in the world the moment it occurs, doctors perform lifesaving operations on unborn babies, McDonald's has served over 99 billion hamburgers, and the list goes on. We can do marvelous things within the laws that govern our physical world, but despite all of our achievements, we are unable to change or break those laws.

However, there is one person who is not bound by physical impossibilities: Jesus Christ. As God, He can do anything, He knows everything, and He is everywhere at the same time. In addition to paying for our sins and teaching about the Christian life, Jesus demonstrated God's power. The miracles that He performed while on earth show that there is no limit to what God can do. Through Jesus, God healed the sick, delivered people from demons, raised people from the dead, and even turned water into wine. These miracles make interesting reading, but why He did them and what we can learn about God from them is even more exciting.

A Demonstration of God's Love

Jesus' mission on earth was threefold: to offer His life as a sacrifice for sin, to show us the character and nature of God, and to show us how He wants us to live. Miracles helped accomplish the second goal. You can use these miracles of Jesus to teach your children how much God loves them and how He wants to work on their behalf. By performing miracles, Jesus showed people two important things about God. First, God loved them. Jesus didn't just parachute out of the clouds, announce that God loved everybody, and expect everyone to love Him in return. Instead, Jesus demonstrated God's love by healing people, setting them free, taking care of their physical needs, and even raising them from the dead. In each of these instances, He saw a human need and responded out of love and compassion. The second thing Jesus' miracles demonstrated was that God is the ultimate power in the universe. There is no disease, power, or event that God does not have authority over, and no want or need too big—or too small—for Him to fulfill.

He Still Moves Stones

God didn't stop doing miracles once He removed the stone from Jesus' tomb or after Jesus returned to heaven. He's still very much at work in the world today, healing, feeding, delivering, and protecting His people. God has not changed, and miracles still can and do happen. However, He has established natural principles and processes in the world to provide for us and to sustain life. When we go to Him asking for things, He usually works through natural processes to meet our needs and answer our prayers. But this fact does not mean that God can't or won't sidestep His natural laws and go above and beyond our circumstances to supernaturally meet our needs if He chooses to.

Teaching children about Jesus' miracles will build their confidence in God's power and desire to help them. They will learn to go to Him for help and will know that He is willing and more than able to meet all of their needs. In short, the miracles of Jesus show that God's power is unlimited and that He loves using it to help them. Now, that's good news!

Places to Model It!

- Tell your children about times when God has done something amazing for you or someone you know or have heard about. Sharing these experiences with your children is a great way for them to see God's power at work today.

- Show your children that you believe God still does miracles today by constantly bringing both large and small needs before Him and requesting an answer. Don't be afraid to talk to Him about anything and everything, from finding a parking spot to praying that a relative would be healed from cancer. No need is too big or too small for God.

- Share with your children how God helped you in the past with areas that they struggle with now.

67

Tips to Teach It!

Key Bible Verse:

"God did miracles, wonders and signs among you through Jesus. You yourselves know this." (Acts 2:22b)

Key Bible Story:

The story of how Jesus used five little loaves of bread and two fish to miraculously feed more than 5,000 people is a Bible classic. Not only was this act a demonstration of the power of God and the divinity of Jesus, it showed us that God cares for us and will look after our needs in very practical ways. Read this story in Luke 9:12–17 with your children and discuss the following questions.

- Why did Jesus' apostles want to send the people away?

- How did Jesus respond to their request? How do you think the apostles felt about His answer?

- What does this story teach about how God will provide for your needs?

Teachable Moments

- When you're reading about Jesus' miracles, tell your children that God is the same yesterday, today, and forever. He provided for His people in the past, and He still wants to do things for them today.

- When they have a need that is beyond their or your ability to meet, encourage them to talk to God and ask Him to intervene with wisdom or action. Do this with your children until asking for His wisdom and help becomes a reflex action every day, and especially when trouble strikes.

- When your children are sick, pray for them in addition to any medical action you take to restore them to health. Talk to them about how sometimes God heals people immediately through miracles and other times He uses natural means, such as medicine or the way our bodies fight off disease. Either way, God is always the One who heals.

Tools to Do It!

1 The Miracles of Jesus

The Gospels record thirty-five miracles performed by Jesus. Matthew mentions twenty of them, Mark mentions eighteen, Luke records twenty, and John notes seven. These, however, are not all of the miracles Jesus did. Matthew, for example, mentions twelve occasions when He performed a number of miraculous works that went unrecorded (for examples see Matthew 4:23–24; 8:16; 9:35). It seems as if the Gospel writers chose to mention certain miracles for their own unique purposes. The following is a list of the miracles in chronological order, along with where they can be found and a lesson each teaches about God and His love.

- **Turning water into wine**

  Where found: John 2:1–11

  Lesson: God wants to help you in practical, down-to-earth ways.

- **The healing of a rich man's son**

  Where found: John 4:46–54

  Lesson: God will reward your faith in Him.

- **The healing of a lame man at the pool of Bethesda**

  Where found: John 5:1–9

  Lesson: God doesn't always do things the way you expect Him to do them.

- **A miraculous catch of fish**

  Where found: Luke 5:1–11

  Lesson: God can provide for your everyday needs in supernatural ways.

- **An exorcism in the synagogue**

  Where found: Mark 1:23–28; Luke 4:31–36

  Lesson: God has power over evil spirits, and He can set people free from them.

- **The healing of Peter's mother-in-law**

TRIVIA

When Jesus healed the ten lepers, how many came back to thank Him?
One (Luke 17:11–19).

Where found: Matthew 8:14–15; Mark 1:29–31; Luke 4:38–39

Lesson: God can make you feel better when you're sick.

- **The cleansing of a leper**

  Where found: Matthew 8:2–4; Mark 1:40–45; Luke 5:12–16

  Lesson: God is concerned about your health and safety.

- **The healing of a paralytic**

  Where found: Matthew 9:2–8; Mark 2:3–12; Luke 5:18–26

  Lesson: Jesus can forgive your sins, and He has power over the effects of sin in the world.

- **The healing of a man with a shriveled hand**

  Where found: Matthew 12:9–13; Mark 3:1–5; Luke 6:6–10

  Lesson: God is concerned with your well-being.

- **The healing of a centurion's servant**

  Where found: Matthew 8:5–13; Luke 7:1–10

  Lesson: When you trust God, you can be sure He'll do what is best for you.

- **The raising of a widow's son**

  Where found: Luke 7:11–15

  Lesson: God cares about the difficult things you go through, and He wants to help.

- **The healing of a man made blind and deaf by a demon**

  Where found: Matthew 12:22

  Lesson: God is more powerful than demons.

- **The calming of the storm**

  Where found: Matthew 8:18, 23–27; Mark 4:35–41; Luke 8:22–25

  Lesson: God has power over nature. You can trust Him, no matter how bad your circumstances appear.

- **The healing of two demon-possessed men**

  Where found: Matthew 8:28–34; Mark 5:1–20; Luke 8:26–39

  Lesson: God is more powerful than demons.

- **The healing of the woman with the bleeding problem**

  Where found: Matthew 9:20–22; Mark 5:25–34; Luke 8:43–48

  Lesson: When you trust God, you can be sure He'll do what's best for you.

- **The raising of Jairus' daughter**

  Where found: Matthew 9:18–19, 23–26; Mark 5:22–24, 35–43; Luke 8:41–42, 49–56

Lesson: God is more powerful than death.

- **The healing of the two blind men**

  Where found: Matthew 9:27–31

  Lesson: When you trust God, you can be sure He'll do what's best for you.

- **The deliverance of a man made mute by a demon**

  Where found: Matthew 9:32–33

  Lesson: God is more powerful than demons.

- **The feeding of the 5,000**

  Where found: Matthew 14:14–21; Mark 6:34–44; Luke 9:12–17; John 6:5–13

  Lesson: God is more than able to meet your needs.

- **Walking on the water**

  Where found: Matthew 14:24–33; Mark 6:45–52; John 6:16–21

  Lesson: God will test your faith.

- **The deliverance of a non-Jew's daughter**

  Where found: Matthew 15:21–28; Mark 7:24–30

  Lesson: God cares about all people in the world.

- **The healing of a deaf and mute man in Decapolis**

  Where found: Mark 7:31–37

  Lesson: God has the power to heal our bodies.

- **The feeding of the 4,000**

  Where found: Matthew 15:32–39; Mark 8:1–9

  Lesson: God is not limited by your resources. He can meet your needs no matter how hopeless things appear.

- **The healing of a blind man at Bethsaida**

  Where found: Mark 8:22–26

  Lesson: God is able to heal.

- **The deliverance of a demon-possessed boy**

  Where found: Matthew 17:14–18; Mark 9:14–29; Luke 9:38–42

  Lesson: Everything is possible for God.

- **The coin in the fish's mouth**

  Where found: Matthew 17:24–27

  Lesson: God provides for your needs in practical ways.

- **The healing of a man born blind**

  Where found: John 9:1–7

TRIVIA

What three people did Jesus raise from the dead during His ministry on earth?

A widow's son (Luke 7:11–15), Jairus's daughter (Matthew 9:18–19, 23–26; Mark 5:22–24, 35–43; Luke 8:41–42, 49–56), and Lazarus (John 11:17–44).

Lesson: God wants to display His power in your life.

- **The healing of a crippled woman on the Sabbath**

  Where found: Luke 13:10–17

  Lesson: God is more concerned with your well-being than with what others think.

- **The healing of a man with a swollen body**

  Where found: Luke 14:1–6

  Lesson: God is more concerned with your well-being than with what others think.

- **The raising of Lazarus**

  Where found: John 11:17–44

  Lesson: God has compassion, and He is more powerful than death.

- **The cleansing of ten lepers**

  Where found: Luke 17:11–19

  Lesson: God has the power to heal you of even the worst diseases.

- **The healing of Bartimaeus**

  Where found: Mark 10:46–52; Luke 18:35–43

  Lesson: When you trust God, He does what is best for you.

- **The cursing of the fig tree**

  Where found: Matthew 21:18–22; Mark 11:12–14, 20–25

  Lesson: God does great things when people have faith in Him.

- **The healing of Malchus's ear**

  Where found: Luke 22:49–51; John 18:10

  Lesson: God does not want anyone to suffer, not even your enemies.

- **A second miraculous catch of fish**

  Where found: John 21:1–11

  Lesson: God reveals Himself through the powerful things He does.

RIDDLE

Once I had two ears, then I had one, then I had two again. Who am I? *Malchus (Luke 22:49–51; John 18:10).*

Celebrating Christmas and Easter

Chapter Nine

Topic

Christmas and Easter: "Holy Days" or "Humbug"?

Knowing who Jesus is and what He has done for us is certainly cause to celebrate with your family. But we live in a culture where Santa Claus and the Easter Bunny have all but taken the place of Jesus when it comes to celebrating Christmas and Easter. When confronted with this fact, it's tempting to say, "Humbug," and choose to have nothing to do with the holidays, rather than go along with these commercial traditions. But just because Christmas and Easter have become highly secularized and commercialized is no reason for Christians to balk at celebrating these events. These "Holy Days" are the two highest celebrations on the Christian calendar.

Rather than take all of the fun out of the holidays for your children or reject them altogether, use the opportunities the holidays provide to emphasize the true reason for the season: the birth, death, and resurrection of Jesus Christ. The more fun you make the celebrations, the more positively the real message behind them will be reinforced to your children.

Christians have more to celebrate during these holidays than anyone else, so celebrate with all your might. Jesus came to earth to set you free from your sins and restore your relationship with God. As a Christian,

you've accepted this wonderful truth, and you have been rewarded with eternal life in heaven (John 3:16). Christmas and Easter are the official days to celebrate the events that made this possible. By celebrating these days with joy and enthusiasm, you demonstrate to your children and others who may be watching your excitement for the message behind them.

The Stories Behind the Symbols

Many people today would be surprised—and possibly shocked—to discover that a number of well-loved Christian hymns, such as "A Mighty Fortress Is Our God," were originally based on the tunes of popular secular songs of the sixteenth century. This was done by church leaders such as Martin Luther to help make the Christian message more relevant to the common people. But does this fact make the songs any less suitable for Christian worship? Not at all.

The same can be said for a number of Christmas and Easter traditions. Children enjoy Santa Claus, presents, Easter eggs, and so on. Just because these symbols are widely used by the secular community does not mean that they are bad and cannot be incorporated into your Christian celebrations. In fact, many of these symbols have Christian roots that have been glossed over through the years. For example, Santa Claus is based on the person of St. Nicholas, the Bishop of Myra (in modern-day Turkey) in the fourth century A.D. Legend has it that Nicholas was a shy but very generous man who went around secretly doing good for the poor and unfortunate. After his death, the stories about him became famous around the world. Over time, they grew into their modern-day versions, and Nicholas's name was changed to Santa Claus, which comes from the word *Sinterklaas*, a Dutch variant of the name "Saint Nicholas." (For more on the stories behind holiday symbols and traditions see Tools to Do It.)

Striking a Balance

For your children's sake, don't totally eliminate the so-called secular traditions from your holiday celebrations. Instead, shift the emphasis back to where it belongs: onto Jesus. Take a balanced approach to your holiday celebrations. Find enjoyable ways to emphasize the true meaning of the season. Build exciting family traditions around them. But let your children also have fun with some of the secular traditions that go along with it (all the while being careful to teach them the difference between "holiday fact" and "holiday fiction"). Your children will thank you for it, and they will be more open to receive the true reason for the season.

Places to Model It!

- Make time to get involved in your church's Christmas and Easter programs. Don't leave programs to the Sunday school and youth group to perform. Set a positive example by taking an active role in these important church celebrations.

- Your family holiday traditions—the decorations and ornaments you cherish, the things you emphasize, and how you decorate your home—all say a lot about what you consider to be central about the holidays. Focus them on the true meaning of the seasons: Jesus Christ and what His life, death, and resurrection mean to us.

- Make the Christian symbols of Christmas and Easter as enjoyable as the secular symbols. An excellent way to do this is to focus your celebrations around historic Christian traditions such as Advent, the twelve days of Christmas, or setting up the nativity scene. For more on how to do this, see Tools to Do It.

- With so much emphasis put on fancy decorations, expensive gifts, Easter eggs, food, and so on, you might be tempted to gripe about the commercialism of the holidays instead of taking a positive attitude toward celebrating Jesus. Instead, take advantage of the opportunities Christmas and Easter provide to have fun with presents, food, parties, and decorations. Don't knock secular ways of celebrating the seasons. Rather, show your excitement about the holidays and what they signify about Jesus.

- Christmas is an excellent time to teach your children about helping people who are less fortunate. Why not take time to get your family involved in a Christmas food hamper or shoebox campaign through your church, or help your local food bank collect or distribute food? When you're doing this, keep in mind that while it is good to teach your children to share with others, this should add to their joy and experience, not be at the expense of it. Instead of saying, "Sorry, kids, you don't get any presents this year because we gave all the money we would have spent on gifts to charity," the time or money you donate to charity should be above and beyond what you do for your children.

MOTTO

Jesus is our reason for really celebrating the season!

Tips to Teach It!

Christmas

Key Bible Verse:

"The people who are now living in darkness will see a great light. They are now living in a very dark land. But a light will shine on them." (Matthew 4:16)

Key Bible Story:

One of the most detailed records of Christ's birth is found in the Gospel of Luke. Read Luke 2:1–20 with your children and discuss the following questions.

- Why do you think Jesus was born in a stable? Do you think that was supposed to happen?

- Why do you think the shepherds were afraid of the angels? Do you think they understood what was going on?

- What does the birth of Jesus mean to you?

Easter

Key Bible Verse:

"What I received I passed on to you. And it is the most important of all. Here is what it is. Christ died for our sins, just as Scripture said he would. He was buried. He was raised from the dead on the third day, just as Scripture said he would be." (1 Corinthians 15:3–4)

Key Bible Story:

The Gospel accounts of Jesus' crucifixion are both disturbing and full of hope. On the one hand, we read about the torture and abuse He experienced during His arrest and trial, and the agony He felt while He hung on the cross. But at the same time, some incredible events were taking place, such as the darkening of the sky, an earthquake, the tearing of the curtain in the temple, and the resurrection of many "holy people." These signs point toward the even more awesome display of God's power that was to come three days later with Jesus' resurrection. Read the account of Jesus' crucifixion and death in Matthew 27:27–56 with your children, then discuss the following questions.

- Why do you think the people were so mean to Jesus before He died?

- Why do you think Jesus asked God why He had forsaken Him? (Note to parents: This cry is thought to reflect how Jesus felt as He bore the sins of the world.)

- What convinced the commander and the other people that Jesus was the Son of God?

- What does Jesus' death mean to you?

Teachable Moments

- It's natural for children to be excited about presents, and you shouldn't put gifts at odds with the true meaning of Christmas. Instead, when your children are getting excited about the approach of Christmas and the presents they will receive, show them how the giving of gifts fits into the Christmas narrative. For example, salvation is the ultimate gift offered to us by God through Jesus. In addition, the wise men brought Jesus gifts when they came to worship Him.

Kids helping kids
Christmas Fund

- Make a family tradition of reading the Christmas and Easter stories. This tradition can be combined with games and food to make it a fun time for everyone. However, doing this on Christmas morning right before gift opening, or on Easter morning right before the Easter egg hunt can backfire because the kids view it as the boring part. Find a time that works for your family and adds to your children's celebration instead of colliding with other parts of it.

- When you're singing Christmas carols together, focus on songs with an explicit Christian message, such as "Away in a Manger," "Silent Night," and "Hark, the Herald Angels Sing." Take time to explain the carols to your children, because they can become so familiar that we forget what we are singing about. Explaining the language can be a natural lead-in to talking about the meaning of the words.

- Establish a "Christmas Giving Fund" that your children can contribute to in the months leading up to Christmas. Then, as you're shopping together for the family's Christmas gifts, they can use this money to purchase presents for people outside the family or for those who are less fortunate than themselves.

- As the holiday seasons approach, make a tradition of watching your family's favorite film about Jesus. You can make this a fun event by including food, friends, games, and discussions. For a list of movies about Jesus, see Tools to Do It.

Tools to Do It!

1 *The Christmas and Easter Stories from the Bible*

Read these stories with your family during the holiday seasons. They will help remind them of the significance of the holiday you are celebrating. By adding prayers, food, and fellowship to the reading, you can turn the event into an eagerly anticipated holiday tradition. They can also become your children's Bible readings in the days leading up to Christmas and Easter.

• *Christmas*

The complete Christmas story with all of the elements in their proper chronological order is presented in the chart below. This story can be read all at once or on separate days leading up to and following Christmas. The Gospels contain different parts of the story. This list allows you to read the whole story using pieces of it taken from Matthew and Luke.

Jesus' birth foretold to Mary	Luke 1:26–38
Mary's visit to Elizabeth	Luke 1:39–45
Mary's song of joy	Luke 1:46–56
Jesus' birth foretold to Joseph	Matthew 1:18–25
The birth of Jesus	Luke 2:1–7
The witness of the shepherds	Luke 2:8–20
The circumcision of Jesus	Luke 2:21
Jesus presented in the temple	Luke 2:22–38
Return to Nazareth	Luke 2:39
Visit of the Magi	Matthew 2:1–12
Flight into Egypt	Matthew 2:13–18
New home in Nazareth	Matthew 2:19–23

• *Easter*

The complete Easter story with all of the elements in proper chronological order is presented in the chart below. This story can be read all at once or on the days leading up to Easter.

The betrayal of Jesus	John 18:2–12
Jesus before Annas	John 18:13–24
Jesus before Caiaphas and the Sanhedrin	Matthew 26:57–68
Peter's denials	John 18:25–27
Jesus before the Sanhedrin	Luke 22:66–71
Judas commits suicide	Matthew 27:3–10
Jesus before Pilate	John 18:28–38
Jesus before Herod Antipas	Luke 23:6–12
Jesus before Pilate again	John 18:39–19:16
Jesus mocked by the soldiers	Mark 15:16–19
Journey to Golgotha	Matthew 27:31–34
The first three hours of crucifixion	John 19:18–27
The last three hours of crucifixion	John 19:28–30
Witness of Jesus' death	Mark 15:38–41
Certification of Jesus' death	John 19:31–38
Jesus' body placed in a tomb	John 19:39–42
Jesus' tomb watched by the women and guarded by soldiers	Matthew 27:61–66
Jesus' tomb found empty	Matthew 28:1–8; John 20:2–10
Jesus appears to Mary Magdalene	John 20:11–18
Jesus appears to the two disciples on the road to Emmaus	Luke 24:13–32
Jesus appears to the disciples	John 20:19–31

TRIVIA

What did Judas do with the money he received for betraying Jesus? *He threw it back at the priests in the temple (Matthew 27:3–5).*

2 *Nativity Scene Activities*

The nativity scene has long been a well-loved tradition in many churches. If you have a nativity scene at home, or if you want to buy or make one, you can use it as the basis for an enjoyable, meaningful family tradition. It will heighten your children's anticipation and appreciation of the meaning behind the Christmas season.

Here's how you do it: On December 22, put up the backdrop of the stable without any of the characters inside. The next day, add the animals. On Christmas Eve, add Mary and Joseph. On Christmas morning, add Jesus in the manger. Later that day, add the shepherds. Then leave the nativity scene unchanged for one week. Finally, on New Year's Eve, you can add the wise men. (This period of waiting stands for the years between when Jesus was born and when the wise men paid their famous visit.)

TRIVIA

What did Jesus do to prove He was not a ghost?

He ate a piece of broiled fish (Luke 24:41–42).

3 *Advent Readings*

The month leading up to Christmas has long been celebrated as a season of preparation for the birth of Jesus. This season of preparation is called Advent. Although not every church marks this tradition, you may want to incorporate it into your family's celebrations. It's a great way to add to the celebrations and bring structure and a sense of "this really happened" to your teaching and storytelling. The following is a series of readings that you can go through on the four Sundays before Christmas and on Christmas Day. Each reading includes an Old Testament prophecy about Jesus and an episode from the story of His birth.

In addition to the readings, many churches light a series of candles to mark the Sundays before Christmas. Depending on what you want to emphasize in your Christmas celebrations, each candle can have a different meaning attached to it. Traditionally, the first candle stands for hope, the second for faith, the third for peace, the fourth for joy, and the fifth for love. Another idea is to have each candle represent a different name for Jesus. Use one or both of these themes, or something else that fits your family's celebrations.

One candle is lit the first Sunday while you are reading the verses for that day. That candle and one more are lit the second Sunday, and so on until Christmas Eve, when all five candles are lit. A good idea is to buy or make an advent wreath that will hold four candles in the ring and one in the middle, and then set it on your table. This can be a beautiful Christmas display. Build anticipation by talking about what you will do ahead of time. Also, combining this tradition with a special evening Christmas snack will make it even more fun for your children.

Day	Old Testament Reading	New Testament Reading
First Sunday	Genesis 3:15	Galatians 4:4–7
Second Sunday	Micah 5:2	Matthew 2:1–5

Third Sunday	Isaiah 7:14	Matthew 1:18–25; Luke 1:26–38
Fourth Sunday	Jeremiah 23:5–6	John 3:16–21
Christmas Eve	Isaiah 59:15b–21	Luke 1:67–80

Note: It is a good idea to read through these Scriptures beforehand and come up with a few discussion questions that you can talk about with your children.

4 Easter Readings

The week leading up to Easter has traditionally been known as Holy Week. We've included a list of readings that you may want to read with your family each day of this week in order to heighten their appreciation of the significance of the Easter season. We've also included a post-Easter reading to help celebrate the victory over sin and death that Jesus won on the cross.

Day	Old Testament Reading	New Testament Reading
Sunday	Zechariah 9:9–12	Luke 19:28–44
Monday	Psalm 69:7–9; Isaiah 56:7	Luke 19:45–48
Tuesday	Psalm 118:22–23; Isaiah 8:14–15; 28:16	Luke 20:1–18
Wednesday	Psalm 41:9	Luke 22:1–6
Thursday	Isaiah 55:3–4; Jeremiah 31:31–33	Luke 22:7–54
Friday	Isaiah 53:7–12	Luke 22:54–23:55
Saturday	Jonah 1:17–2:10	Luke 23:56
Sunday	Psalm 16:9–11	Luke 24

Note: Again, it is a good idea to read through these Scriptures beforehand and come up with a few discussion questions that you can talk about with your children.

5 The Twelve Days of Christmas

Most people are familiar with the Christmas carol "The Twelve Days of Christmas", but few people know the story behind it.

The "Twelve Days of Christmas" is actually a catechism song (a song that explains basic Christian beliefs). Between 1558 and 1829, Catholics in England were not allowed to practice their faith openly. Without regular church services or lessons from the priest, there was little parents could do to help their children learn all about their faith. "The Twelve

TRIVIA

Why did Mary and Joseph have to travel to Bethlehem?
To register for the census (Luke 2:1–4).

Days of Christmas" was created to keep the Catholic faith in their lives, even though it remained hidden.

The song was written in code. For example, instead of referring to a boyfriend or a girlfriend, the "true love" mentioned in the song refers to God. The "me" who receives the present is a symbol for every Christian. "A partridge in a pear tree" is Jesus. This is because a mother partridge will fake an injury to decoy predators from her babies so that she would die instead of them. The children who heard this song would know that and would understand the parallel between the acts of a mother partridge and the sacrifice Jesus made on the cross. The other words in the song continue the symbolism:

- Two turtledoves = The Old and New Testaments

- Three French hens = Faith, hope, and love

- Four calling birds = The four Gospels

- Five golden rings = The first five books of the Old Testament (Genesis, Exodus, Leviticus, Numbers, and Deuteronomy), which give the history of humankind's fall from grace and the beginning of God's solution

- Six geese a-laying = The six days of Creation

- Seven swans a-swimming = Seven gifts of the Holy Spirit

- Eight maids a-milking = The eight Beatitudes

- Nine ladies dancing = Nine choirs of angels

- Ten lords a-leaping = The Ten Commandments

- Eleven pipers piping = The eleven faithful apostles

- Twelve drummers drumming = The twelve points of belief in the Apostles' Creed

6 *Holiday Symbols and Their Meanings*

Following are the histories and meanings of several popular Christmas and Easter traditions. A number of these traditions have deep Christian roots. Share these stories with your children as a way of helping them get a proper perspective on the traditions.

• *Christmas*

Gifts: The tradition of giving gifts at Christmastime was inspired by the gifts that the wise men gave to Jesus. However, the habit of exchanging gifts the way we know it today did not start in Europe and North America until the late 1800s. The legend of Santa Claus combined with the push of retailers has now made gift giving a central focus of the Christmas season.

You can help your children maintain the right focus on gifts by showing them how much fun it is to come up with creative gift ideas for others. Put the emphasis on giving and receiving love, and how their gifts show their love to others.

Christmas Tree: In the seventh century, a monk from Crediton, Devonshire, went to Germany to teach the Word of God. Legend has it that he used the triangular shape of the fir tree to describe the Trinity—God the Father, Son, and Holy Spirit. The converted people began to revere the fir tree as God's tree. By the twelfth century in central Europe it was being hung upside-down from ceilings at Christmas time as a symbol of Christianity.

The first decorated Chrismas tree was at Riga, Latvia, in 1510. In the last part of the sixteenth century, Martin Luther is said to have decorated a small tree with candles to show his children how the stars twinkled through the dark on the night Jesus was born. The Christmas tree really came into its own in the mid-1800s when Prince Albert, who was from Germany where the custom was common, set up a Christmas tree in England. The custom of decorating and lighting Christmas trees spread quickly throughout England and North America. Tiny lightbulbs began to replace candles on Christmas trees in the early part of the twentieth century.

Holly: The church originally introduced holly as a Christmas tradition to replace the use of mistletoe—which was shunned because of its association with pagan rituals and idolatry in Europe. The sharply pointed leaves of the holly were to symbolize the thorns in Christ's crown during His trial, and the red berries were to symbolize drops of His blood.

Stockings: This tradition goes back to a legend about St. Nicholas. According to the story, a poor man couldn't provide a dowry for his three daughters to get married. One night, Nicholas secretly dropped a bag of gold into an open window of the man's house. This money provided enough dowry for the oldest daughter to be married. Nicholas repeated his gift for the second daughter, and she too was married. When Nicholas tossed in the third bag of gold, one legend says it landed in one of the third daughter's stockings, which had been hung by the fire to dry. Thus the tradition began. This is a fascinating story to illustrate to your children the concept of "giving" at Christmas.

RIDDLE

Where in Bethlehem did the wise men find Jesus?

You may be suprised to learn that the wise men found Jesus in a house in Bethlehem as a young child, not in a manger as a newborn baby (Matthew 2:11).

• *Easter*

The Easter Bunny: Like the egg, rabbits have long been considered symbols of fertility and new life during the spring season. The bunny was first mentioned as an Easter symbol in Germany during the 1500s. It stood for the new life we have in Jesus once we become Christians. The first edible Easter bunnies were also made in Germany during the early 1800s. They were made of pastry and sugar. The Easter bunny was introduced to America by German settlers who arrived in Pennsylvania in the 1700s. Children believed that if they were good, the Easter bunny, or the *Oschter Haws* as it is called in German, would lay a nest of colored eggs.

Easter Eggs: For centuries, the egg has been a powerful symbol of fertility and new life. In many parts of Europe, decorated eggs were buried in newly planted fields and hung from fruit trees during

Easter week to assure good crops. People believed the eggs had special powers to help them in their daily life. Eggs later became associated with the new life we have in Jesus, and they were often decorated with pictures of Jesus, the Virgin Mary, and other Christian designs. Today, different cultures have developed their own ways of decorating Easter eggs. Crimson eggs, to honor the blood of Jesus, are exchanged in Greece. In parts of Germany and Austria, green eggs are exchanged on Maundy Thursday. (Maundy is another word for "Holy.") Ukrainians and other Slavic peoples make beautiful "Pysanki" eggs, which are decorated with intricate patterns made with dyes and beeswax.

Jesus Was a Kid, Too

Topic

Been There, Done That

"But you don't understand!" is a familiar cry heard from children. The trials and frustrations children go through from day to day may appear so overwhelming that they are convinced no one can understand their pain and suffering—even if the problem is nothing more than a squabble with a friend or a term paper that needs to be completed by next week. Little do your children suspect that you were a child once, too, and you can identify with everything they're going through, from social "disasters" to homework blues.

Adults often talk about how Jesus can identify with us as our high priest because, as the book of Hebrews says, He faced the same struggles and temptations we face today. *"We have a high priest who can feel it when we are weak and hurting. We have a high priest who has been tempted in every way, just as we are. But he did not sin"* (Hebrews 4:15). But what is seldom emphasized is that Jesus was also a child at one time. He is not only your children's Savior and teacher, He's their high priest as well. And He can identify with everything they are going through.

His Father's Son

Jesus is the Son of God, but while He lived on earth He was also the adopted son of Joseph. Joseph was a carpenter, and, according to the Jewish way of life back then, he probably trained Jesus to work with him in his shop from a young age. Jesus would have learned how to make furniture, tools, wheels, and so on.

In addition, Jesus probably attended school, went to the synagogue (a Jewish church), did chores, played with His siblings and friends, and spent time with His relatives. During this time He would have gone through many struggles and temptations, just as children do today. For example, He would have had to obey His father and mother, even if it meant sacrificing time with His friends. Matthew 13:55 indicates that Jesus had at least four brothers, and He would certainly have had to deal with times when they were difficult to get along with. In other words, on a very basic level, Jesus' life as a child was not significantly different from the life of your children today.

Guidance for Life

So the next time the children complain that you just don't understand what they're going through, direct them to Jesus, and explain how they can look to Him for help and guidance at every stage of their lives. They can be assured that He both knows what they are going through and is more than willing to help. All your children need to do is ask.

TRIVIA

Where in the Bible do we read that Jesus was tempted just as we are? *Hebrews 4:15.*

Places to Model It!

- Demonstrate with your life that you know God understands and cares about everything you're going through. You can do this by taking everything to Him in prayer and verbalizing your belief that He will help you.

- When you ask God for help, He doesn't just give you the right information to fix the problem and then send you on your way. He is compassionate toward you, and He helps you lovingly. Take this approach when helping your children with problems they are experiencing. If they are having trouble understanding how to solve a mathematical problem, don't just quickly explain how to do it and then send them on their way. Instead, sit down and listen to what aspect of the problem they're struggling with, explain how to solve the problem, supervise while they work through it, and stick with them until they solve it. When you let your children know that this is how God helps them, too, their faith will grow.

- As a child, it is likely that you went through nearly everything your children are going through right now. Take a moment to recall how you felt and what you struggled with. Relate to your children on this basis, and show them how Jesus understands them even better than you do.

Tips to Teach It!

Key Bible Verse:

"Then he [Jesus] went back to Nazareth with them, and he obeyed them . . . Jesus became wiser and stronger. He also became more and more pleasing to God and to people." (Luke 2:51–52)

Key Bible Story:

Apart from the account of His birth, the story of Jesus in the temple is the only glimpse we get of His life as a child. But even this brief episode is enough to demonstrate that He can identify with and understand what children go through. Read Luke 2:41–52 with your children and discuss the following questions.

- Why do you think Jesus stayed behind in Jerusalem?

- What did Jesus mean when He said, "Didn't you know I had to be in my Father's house?"

- What does this story teach you about children and God?

Teachable Moments

- When your children are having a difficult time with their friends, or they're feeling frustrated and powerless because they are not old enough to do what they want, encourage them to believe that God understands what they are going through. As Jesus, He was once a child, too, and He had many of the same struggles as your children. Encourage them to take their frustrations to God.

- When you're reading the story of Jesus in the temple, encourage your children to apply themselves to seeking and getting to know God at a young age as Jesus did. He knew what He knew—which was enough to amaze the religious leaders—because He trusted God and sought His wisdom and understanding. He was God, yes, but he was also human. And as a human child He trusted God the Father to teach Him—just as every child needs to.

- If your children have questions about Jesus or the Bible, praise them and encourage them as they search for answers. Help them in their search.

Tools to Do It!

1 *Jesus in the Temple*

There are a number of elements in the story of Jesus as a child in the temple that children today can understand and relate to their own experiences. The following commentary on the story and the discussion questions will help you pull out and discuss aspects of the story that your children can relate to.

"Every year Jesus' parents went to Jerusalem for the Passover Feast. When he was 12 years old, they went up to the Feast as usual." (Luke 2:41)

- Jesus needed to attend church and other special functions with His parents.

- Jesus had to take time away from some of the many activities He enjoyed at home.

- Jesus obeyed His parents and respected their desire for Him to accompany them on the trip.

Questions:

- Why did Jesus' family go to Jerusalem?

- How do you think Jesus felt about going on the trip?

- Are there ever times when you have to go somewhere with your parents, even if you don't want to?

"After the Feast was over, his parents left to go back home. The boy Jesus stayed behind in Jerusalem. But they were not aware of it. They thought he was somewhere in their group. So they traveled on for a day. Then they began to look for him among their relatives and friends. They did not find him. So they went back to Jerusalem to look for him." (Luke 2:43–45)

MOTTO

Jesus knows what I'm going through, and He wants to help.

- Jesus grew up in community with other people, and He had to learn how to get along with them.

- Jesus spent time with His friends and relatives.

- Jesus went on holidays with His family.

Questions:

- Why do you think it took so long for Mary and Joseph to discover that Jesus was missing?

- How do you think Jesus' parents felt when they found out He wasn't with them?

- Have you ever been lost? How did it feel?

> *"After three days they found him in the temple courtyard. He was sitting with the teachers. He was listening to them and asking them questions. Everyone who heard him was amazed at how much he understood. They also were amazed at his answers. When his parents saw him, they were amazed."* **(Luke 2:46–48a)**

- Jesus wanted to do something different from what His parents did.

- Jesus wanted to do a grown-up thing.

- Jesus sought out God and His wisdom at a young age.

- Jesus was not afraid to ask questions if He wanted to know something.

Questions:

- What was Jesus doing when His parents found Him in the temple?

- What did the teachers and other people at the temple think of Jesus?

- Do you think Jesus was too young to be asking about God? Why or why not?

> *"His mother said to him, 'Son, why have you treated us like this? Your father and I have been worried about you. We have been looking for you everywhere.' 'Why were you looking for me?' he asked. 'Didn't you know I had to be in my Father's house?' But they did not understand what he meant by that."* (Luke 2:48b–50) *She'd been worried about her child, and now that she had found Him, she wanted to know what He'd been doing.*

- Mary was just like any other mother.

- Jesus was sometimes misunderstood by His parents.

TRIVIA

What were the names of Jesus' brothers?

James, Joseph, Simon, and Judas (Matthew 13:55).

RIDDLE

God told me that I wouldn't die until after I had seen the Messiah. Who am I?

Simeon (Luke 2:25–35).

Questions:

- Why did Jesus tell His mother that He was in His Father's house?

- It doesn't seem that Jesus' parents understood Him at this point. Can you think of a time when you thought your parents didn't understand you? How did that feel?

"Then he went back to Nazareth with them, and he obeyed them. But his mother kept all these things like a secret treasure in her heart." (Luke 2:51)

- Sometimes Jesus had to stop doing something He enjoyed because His parents asked Him to.

- Jesus was obedient to His parents and trusted their leadership.

Questions:

- What did Jesus do when He went back to Nazareth?

- What did his mother think of everything that had happened?

- Think about a time when you were doing something fun and your parents asked you to come home with them. How did that feel? Did you obey them? Why or why not?

"Jesus became wiser and stronger. He also became more and more pleasing to God and to people." (Luke 2:52)

- Jesus had to grow up.

- Jesus had to learn wisdom.

- Jesus had to learn how to please God.

- Jesus had to get along with others in His community.

Questions:

- What do you think made Jesus wiser?

- Why do you think Jesus became more pleasing to God and to people?

- What can you do to become wiser and more pleasing to God and people?

TRIVIA

What trade did Jesus learn while growing up? *Carpentry (Mark 6:3).*

Chapter Eleven

Sharing Your Faith in Jesus

Topic

Share the Good News

There's nothing better than having good news to share. Whether you've just found out you're going to have a baby or you just bought a new car, the first thing you want to do is tell someone. Your children will feel the same way when they come to know Jesus and understand how wonderful, loving, and understanding He is. Through Jesus they gain forgiveness for their sins, eternal life with God after they die, and a direct link to Him right here and now. It's only natural to want to share this good news with friends and family. Not only will they want to tell others about their relationship with God, but Jesus has told them to do it: *"So you must go and make disciples of all nations . . . Teach them to obey everything I have commanded you. And you can be sure that I am always with you, to the very end"* (Matthew 28:19–20). This passage is called the "Great Commission," and it is the mandate for all Christians everywhere.

Live It Out

A Bible passage that explains how you and your children can share your faith effectively is 1 Peter 3:15–16: *"But make sure in your hearts that Christ is Lord. Always be ready to give an answer to anyone who asks you about the hope you have. Be ready to give the reason for it. But do it gently and with respect. Live so that you don't have to feel you've done anything wrong. Some people may say evil things about your good conduct as believers in Christ. If they do, they will be put to shame for speaking like that about you."*

This passage explains that before you tell others about Jesus, you must first make Him the Lord, or Master, of your own life. Next, you should always be prepared to explain why you believe what you do. This telling others about Jesus is called "evangelism."

This passage also says that *how* you tell others about Jesus, and how you live in general, is as important as *what* you tell others about Him. Showing others that Jesus is real through the way you talk and live is called "witnessing." Whether you and your children are conscious of it or not, your character, values, attitude, and approach to life are broadcasting a message to others about your relationship with God. If you obey Jesus, people will notice how you live and wonder about it. Sooner or later they will begin to make the connection between your faith, your actions, and your life, and they will start asking questions.

Encourage Your Children

Your children need as much encouragement as you do when it comes to expressing their faith, if not more. Being regarded as different from their peers is not an enviable position among children or teens. Explain to them that, as they pray for others and live God's way, witnessing and evangelism will be a natural outgrowth of these activities. God will supply many opportunities "in the middle of life" for them to tell others about Jesus. Teach your children that this should always be done with meekness and respect. They should never argue about Christianity or force others into a decision. Although God wants to have a relationship with everyone, each person is free to make his or her own choice. They can pray for people, but the choice of whether or not to follow God is ultimately that person's. God respects that, and so must your children.

TRIVIA

What does the word "Gospel" mean?

Good news.

Places to Model It!

- Be a witness for Christ wherever you go. This doesn't mean you have to stand on the street corner waving a Bible and preaching to the masses. It just means modeling the character of Christ in every situation you find yourself in. Don't shy away from opportunities to let friends and strangers know that you're a Christian. For example, if you have non-Christian friends over for supper, don't be afraid to say grace before the meal, and don't be afraid to tell them why you do it.

- If you're out shopping, visiting a museum, or walking in the park, and someone makes a comment to you about God or Christianity, don't shy away from the topic. It may be an opportunity that God is opening up. It's definitely an opportunity to show your kids that you are not ashamed of being a Christian. Be natural about it, though. And be careful to stay away from Christian terms or catch phrases that non-Christians won't understand.

- Build the teachings and character of Jesus into your own life. Let these traits be a beacon to call people to Jesus. Be thankful, forgiving, loving, and merciful. Make Christ's character your character.

- Take every opportunity to talk to others about Jesus. Later, tell your children about the situation and how it went. Explain how you answered the person's questions, what Scriptures you used, and how the person responded. This will help your children learn how they should respond when they are asked about their faith.

Tips to Teach It!

Key Verse

"But make sure in your hearts that Christ is Lord. Always be ready to give an answer to anyone who asks you about the hope you have. Be ready to give the reason for it. But do it gently and with respect." (1 Peter 3:15)

Key Bible Story

As a missionary, Paul devoted his life to telling others of Jesus. In Acts 17:15–34, he found himself in Athens—and in the midst of a tremendous witnessing opportunity. Read the story with your children and discuss the following questions.

- What did Paul see in Athens that troubled him?

- What did he do about it?

- What was the result?

- What are some ways you can tell others about Jesus? Be specific.

Teachable Moments

- Encourage your children to be ready to respond to questions about their faith as they come up. For example, if their non-Christian friends are over for supper and they ask why you say grace before the meal, have your children simply and matter-of-factly explain that grace is just your way of saying thanks to God for everything He's given you.

- When they are choosing their friends, help them understand the difference between close friendships and other relationships. It is good to have non-Christian friends, but their closest friends should be Christians who share their faith and values. This is because Christian friends and your children can encourage each other to grow spiritually. Together they can be a positive influence on their non-Christian friends.

- Encourage your children to think of ways to speak of their faith to their non-Christian friends. For example, if they are going out to a fun church activity, encourage them to invite one or two non-Christian friends along. Building positive relationships with others is one of the best ways to show God's love.

- When their friends have questions about Christianity, help your children find answers for them in the Bible. Make sure your children understand the answer and know where to find it so they can show their friends that what they're saying is not just their own words: it's from the Bible. Encourage them to memorize verses (such as the ones in the Tools to Do It section below) so that they will always be ready to give an answer for what they believe, whether they have a Bible handy or not.

- If your children get discouraged because they haven't led anyone to Jesus, or they're afraid to talk about their faith, remind them of the apostle Paul's words in 1 Corinthians 3:5–8: "*After all, what is Apollos? And what is Paul? We are only people who serve. We helped you to believe. The Lord has given each of us our own work to do. I planted the seed. Apollos watered it. But God made it grow. So the one who plants is not important. The one who waters is not important. It is God who makes things grow. He is the One who is important.*" Coming to know Jesus is a process, and you're obeying the Great Commission if what you say or how you live moves even one person a step closer to accepting Him. Your children may introduce one of their friends to one aspect of Jesus or Christianity, but it may take years before the person receives Him as their Lord and Savior. But if it weren't for their telling their friend about Jesus in the first place, the friend might never have become a believer. They can be excited that every Christian has an important role to play in sharing Jesus with the world.

TRIVIA

How should we tell others about Jesus?
With gentleness and respect (1 Peter 3:15).

Tools to Do It!

1 *Memory Verses to Help You Share the Gospel*

RIDDLE

I was a Pharisee who came to visit Jesus one night and ask Him about His teachings. Who am I?

Nicodemus (John 3:1–21).

Assist your children in learning and memorizing the following verses so they can share them with their friends when they have questions about how to become a Christian. Perhaps your children can mark these verses in their Bibles so they know where they are.

- Adam and Eve, the first people, chose to disobey God. After that, everyone was born sinful.

    "Everyone has sinned. No one measures up to God's glory." (Romans 3:23)

    "Sin entered the world because one man sinned. And death came because of sin. Everyone sinned, so death came to all people." (Romans 5:12)

- The penalty for sin is death.

    "When you sin, the pay you get is death. But God gives you the gift of eternal life because of what Christ Jesus our Lord has done." (Romans 6:23)

- But God had a plan in place to help us overcome sin and its penalties.

    "Many people were made sinners because one man [Adam] did not obey. But one man [Jesus] did obey. That is why many people will be made right with God." (Romans 5:19)

    "God loved the world so much that he gave his one and only Son. Anyone who believes in him will not die but will have eternal life." (John 3:16)

    "But here is how God has shown his love for us. While we were still sinners, Christ died for us. The blood of Christ has made us right with God. So we are even more sure that Jesus will save us from God's anger." (Romans 5:8–9)

MOTTO

My life and words will help others know about Jesus.

- We can have a part in what God has done for us by accepting Jesus as our Master and Savior.

    "Say with your mouth, 'Jesus is Lord.' Believe in your heart that God raised him from the dead. Then you will be saved. With your heart you believe and are made right with God. With your mouth you say that Jesus is Lord. And so you are saved." (Romans 10:9–10)

- Salvation is a free gift from God to us. There's nothing we can do to earn it.

  "God's grace has saved you because of your faith in Christ. Your salvation doesn't come from anything you do. It is God's gift. It is not based on anything you have done. No one can brag about earning it." (Ephesians 2:8–9)

2 Common Questions

For answers to commonly asked questions about Christianity, such as "How do we know God is real?" see pages 101–104 in *Your Child and the Christian Life*, another book in this series.

TRIVIA

Where in the Bible do we find "The Great Commission"? *Matthew 28:19–20.*

Engraved Hearts

Engraved Hearts

By now this book should have helped you see how easy it is to teach your children about Jesus, right in the middle of life. Once you are accustomed to bringing Jesus, His story, character, teachings, miracles, and understanding into the different parts of life, you'll find an increasing number of opportunities to keep doing it. God wants your children to know His Son, and He will help you as you seek to teach them about Him. He'll bring opportunities to your notice. God is right alongside you, wanting your children to learn just as much as you do—and more!

God has said, *"I will put my law in their minds. I will write it on their hearts. I will be their God. And they will be my people"* (Jeremiah 31:33). It is His pleasure to help you engrave His laws, His truths, and His love on your children's hearts. He is committed to it.

An Integral Part of Life

As you've seen, the key to this heart-engraving is to make your relationship with Jesus the center of your own life. Jesus is as real, alive, and

17-07

relevant now as He was when He walked the earth. He must become the basis of everything you do, say, and think. Spending time with Him in prayer, learning about His life and teachings, and putting them into practice is what life is all about. This means constantly bringing Jesus into the situations your children encounter every day. Anchor all of your life lessons in God's Word.

Be careful not to bring up Jesus only during serious times. God invented fun. Make learning about Jesus and His ways attractive to your children. When you turn learning into an adventure, they will eagerly look forward to it. Make Jesus, His teachings, His story, and His gift of salvation a natural part of your everyday routine. If you're just beginning to introduce your family to Jesus, start small and build slowly. A good first step is to sit down and talk to the children about what you want to do.

Keep It Exciting

Kids love adventure and variety. Don't fall into a rut with your devotional or training times. With younger kids, consider buying or renting some animated Bible story videos and using them for a special once-a-week event. Use a Bible storybook on CD-ROM for a few nights, or an inspirational story, or a movie based on the Gospels. If at any time your children start to get bored or begin to lose interest in the process, examine your presentation and change what you are doing to raise the excitement level again. Use your imagination. Almost anything goes as long as the learning grows.

As we close, we trust this book has helped you to teach your children about Jesus, who He is, what He's done for them, and how they can have a relationship with Him. Remember: Solid truths instilled today will serve your children throughout their lifetime. *"Train a child in the way he should go. When he is old, he will not turn away from it"* (Proverbs 22:6). Introduce your children to Jesus, and you will have introduced them to the most fruitful relationship of their lives.

Resource List

Resources for Parents

McDowell, Josh. *The Best of Josh McDowell: A Ready Defense.* Nashville: Thomas Nelson, 1993.

———. *Evidence That Demands a Verdict.* San Bernardino: Campus Crusade for Christ, 1972.

———. *More Than a Carpenter.* Wheaton: Tyndale House, 1985.

Morrison, Frank. *Who Moved the Stone?* Grand Rapids: Zondervan, 1987.

Resources for Children

Bible Storybooks (ages 3–7)

Beers, V. Gilbert. *The Toddlers Bible.* Colorado Springs: Chariot, 1992.

Carlson, Melody. *The Golden Honey Bible.* Sisters, Ore.: Gold 'N' Honey Books, 1997.

Currie, Robin. *The Baby Bible Storybook.* Colorado Springs: Chariot, 1994.

Lindvall, Ella K. *The Bible Illustrated for Little Children.* Chicago: Moody, 1987.

———. *Read-Aloud Bible Stories. Vols. 1 (1982), 2 (1985), 3 (1990), 4 (1995).* Chicago: Moody.

Psalty's Kids Bible. Grand Rapids: Zondervan, 1991.

Rikkers, Doris, and Jean E. Syswerda, eds. *Read with Me Bible.* Grand Rapids: Zondervan, 1993.

Syswerda, Jean E., ed. *The Adventure Bible.* Grand Rapids: Zondervan, 1989.

Taylor, Kenneth N. *The Bible in Pictures for Little Eyes.* Chicago: Moody, 1956, 1984.

Bibles for Middle-Grade Children (ages 8–12)

DeJonge, Joanne E. *Kids' Devotional Bible (NIrV).* Grand Rapids: Zondervan, 1996.

Grispino, Joseph A., et al. *The Golden Children's Bible.* New York: Golden Books, 1993.

International Children's Bible. Dallas: Word Bibles, 1988.

The Treasure Study Bible. Indianapolis: Kirkbride, 1998.

Bibles for Teens

PC Study Bible. Seattle: Biblesoft, 1995.

Peterson, Eugene H. *The Message (New Testament in Contemporary English).* Colorado Springs: Nav Press, 1993.

Richards, Larry and Sue Richards. *The Teen Study Bible (NIV).* Grand Rapids: Zondervan, 1993.

The Student Bible (NIV). Grand Rapids: Zondervan, 1996.

The Student's Life Application Bible. Wheaton: Tyndale House, 1997.

WWJD? Resources

Courrege, Beverly. *Answers to: What Would Jesus Do?* Cincinnati: Honor Books, 1997.

Morris, Deborah, and Garrett Ward Sheldon. *What Would Jesus Do? Vols 1 (1993), 2 (1995).* Nashville: Broadman and Holman.

Sheldon, Charles Monroe, et al. *In His Steps, What Would Jesus Do?* Cincinnati: Honor Books, 1998. (For parents)

Thomas, Mack, et al. *What Would Jesus Do?* Sisters, Ore.: Multnomah, 1997. (For children ages 4–8)

The WWJD? Game. Wheaton: Tyndale, 1998.

The Chronicles of Narnia

(The books in this series are listed in the order they are to be read.)

Lewis, C. S. *The Magician's Nephew.* London: Fontana Lions, 1980.

———. *The Lion, the Witch, and the Wardrobe.* London: Fontana Lions, 1980.

———. *The Horse and His Boy.* London: Fontana Lions, 1980.

———. *Prince Caspian.* London: Fontana Lions, 1980.

———. *The Voyage of the Dawntreader.* London: Fontana Lions, 1980.

———. *The Silver Chair.* London: Fontana Lions, 1980.

———. *The Last Battle.* London: Fontana Lions, 1980.

Videos About Jesus

Ben Hur

This classic film starring Charlton Heston is a fictional story that takes place in Jerusalem and Rome during Jesus' time. Although Jesus is instrumental to the plot of the film, He does not play a central role. This movie is an excellent introduction to the life and times of Jesus. For all ages.

Jesus of Nazareth

This movie is perhaps the most moving and graphic account of the life of Jesus ever filmed.

Clocking in at around six hours, this film is also the most detailed of all the movies about Jesus.

Not recommended for very young children.

The Animated Stories from the New Testament

This high quality animated video series from Family Entertainment Network chronicles episodes from the life of Jesus and the growth of the early church. This series will serve as an excellent introduction to the story of Jesus for your children.

The Jesus Film

This is the world-famous film about Jesus made by Campus Crusade for Christ and shown in hundreds of countries and dozens of languages. For all ages.

The Storykeepers

This is a Focus on the Family series of animated videos for children that tells fictional stories of early Christians and their struggles as they attempt to live out their faith. Each video also includes stories from the life of Jesus.

*Lightwave Resource

Lightwave Resources

Other Books in the Learning for Life Series

Osborne, Rick, with K. Christie Bowler. *Your Child and the Christian Life.* Chicago: Moody, 1999.

Osborne, Rick, with Kevin Miller. *Your Child and the Bible.* Chicago: Moody, 1999.

Resources for Teens and Children

Burkett, L. Allen, and Lauree Burkett, with Marnie Wooding. *Money Matters for Teens.* Chicago: Moody, 1997. (Ages 11–18)

Burkett, Larry, with Lauree Burkett. *What If I Owned Everything?* Nashville: Tommy Nelson, 1997. (Ages 3–8)

Burkett, Larry, with Todd Temple. *Money Matters for Teens Workbook.* Chicago: Moody, 1998. (Ages 11–14 and 15–18 editions).

Burkett, Lauree, and L. Allen Burkett. *50 Money Making Ideas for Kids.* Nashville: Tommy Nelson, 1997. (Ages 8 and up)

Burkett, Lauree and K. Christie Bowler. *Money Matters for Kids.* Chicago: Moody, 1997. (Ages 8–10)

Lambier, Doug, and Robert Stevenson. *Genesis for Kids.* Nashville: Tommy Nelson, 1997. (Ages 8–14)

Osborne, Rick, with Ed Strauss and Kevin Miller. *Kidcordance.* Grand Rapids: Zonderkidz, 1999. (Ages 8–12)

Osborne, Rick, with K. Christie Bowler. *I Want to Know About the Bible.* Grand Rapids: Zondervan, 1998. (Ages 8–12)

———. *I Want to Know About God.* Grand Rapids: Zondervan, 1998. (Ages 8–12)

———. *I Want to Know About Jesus.* Grand Rapids: Zondervan, 1998. (Ages 8–12)

———. *I Want to Know About Prayer.* Grand Rapids: Zondervan, 1998. (Ages 8–12)

———. *I Want to Know About the Church.* Grand Rapids: Zondervan, 1998. (Ages 8–12)

———. *I Want to Know About the Holy Spirit.* Grand Rapids: Zondervan, 1998. (Ages 8–12)

———. *I Want to Know About the Ten Commandments.* Grand Rapids: Zonderkidz, 1998. (Ages 8–12)

———. *I Want to Know About the Fruit of the Spirit.* Grand Rapids: Zonderkidz, 1999. (ages 8–12)

Osborne, Rick, and Elaine Osborne. *The Singing Bible.* Nashville: Word, 1993. (Audiotape; ages 4–10).

van der Maas, Ed M. *Adventure Bible Handbook.* Grand Rapids: Zondervan, 1994. (Ages 8–12)

Various authors. "Lightwave Kids' Club (Issues 1–7)." Maple Ridge, BC: Lightwave, 1996. (Ages 8–12)

Lightwave creative team. *The Amazing Treasure Bible Storybook.* Grand Rapids: Zondervan, 1997. (Ages 8–12)

Resources for Parents

Burkett, Larry, and Rick Osborne. *Financial Parenting.* Colorado Springs: Chariot, 1996.

———. *Your Child Wonderfully Made.* Chicago: Moody, 1998.

———. *Financial Parenting.* Chicago: Moody, 1999.

Lucas, Daryl J., gen. ed. *105 Questions Children Ask About Money Matters*. Wheaton, Ill.: Tyndale, 1997.

Osborne, Rick. *Teaching Your Child How to Pray*. Chicago: Moody, 1997.

———. *Talking to Your Children About God*. New York: HarperSanFrancisco, 1998.

Veerman, David R., et al. *101 Questions Children Ask About God*. Wheaton, Ill.: Tyndale, 1992.

———. *102 Questions Children Ask About the Bible*. Wheaton, Ill.: Tyndale, 1994.

———. *103 Questions Children Ask About Right from Wrong*. Wheaton, Ill.: Tyndale, 1995.

———. *104 Questions Children Ask About Heaven and Angels*. Wheaton, Ill.: Tyndale, 1996.

———. *106 Questions Children Ask About Our World*. Wheaton, Ill.: Tyndale, 1998.

———. *107 Questions Children Ask About Prayer*. Wheaton, Ill.: Tyndale, 1998.

———. *108 Questions Children Ask About Friends and School*. Wheaton, Ill.: Tyndale, 1999.

The NIrV Kids' Quest Study Bible. Grand Rapids: Zondervan, 1998.

The WWJD? Game. Wheaton Ill.: Tyndale, 1998.

Games

The Book Game. Wheaton, Ill.: Tyndale, 1999. (Ages 7 and up)

Sticky Situations. Wheaton, Ill.: Tyndale, 1991. (Ages 6 and up)

Money Matters for Kids. Colorado Springs: Rainfall Educational Toys, 1998. (Ages 6–10)

Larry Burkett's Money Matters. Colorado Springs: Rainfall Educational Toys, 1996. (Ages 7 to adult)

L I G H T *wave*

building Christian faith in families

Lightwave Publishing is a recognized leader in developing quality resources that encourage, assist, and equip parents to build Christian faith in their families.

Lightwave Publishing also has a fun kids' Web site and an internet-based newsletter called *Tips & Tools for Spiritual Parenting*. This newsletter helps parents with issues such as answering their children's questions, helping make church more exciting, teaching children how to pray, and much more.

For more information, visit Lightwave's Web site: **www.lightwavepublishing.com**

MOODY
The Name You Can Trust
A MINISTRY OF MOODY BIBLE INSTITUTE

Moody Press, a ministry of Moody Bible Institute, is designed for education, evangelization, and edification.

If we may assist you in knowing more about Christ and the Christian life, please write us without obligation:

Moody Press, c/o MLM
Chicago, Illinois 60610

Or visit us at Moody's Web site: **www.moodypress.org**